The Process Auditing Techniques Guide

The Process Auditing Techniques Guide

J. P. Russell

ASQ Quality Press
Milwaukee, Wisconsin

The Process Auditing Techniques Guide
J.P. Russell

Library of Congress Cataloging-in-Publication Data

Russell, J. P. (James P.), 1945-
   The process auditing techniques guide / J.P. Russell.
      p. cm.
   Includes index.
   ISBN 0-87389-595-9
   1. Auditing. I. Title.

   HF5667.P838 2003
   657'.45--dc21

                                                    2003001459

ISBN 0-87389-595-9

Publisher: William A. Tony
Acquisitions Editor: Annemieke Koudstaal
Project Editor: Paul O'Mara
Production Administrator: Gretchen Trautman
Special Marketing Representative: Robin Barry

ASQ Mission: The American Society for Quality advances individual,
organizational, and community excellence worldwide through learning,
quality improvement, and knowledge exchange.

Attention Bookstores, Wholesalers, Schools, and Corporations: ASQ Quality
Press books, videotapes, audiotapes, and software are available at quantity
discounts with bulk purchases for business, educational, or instructional use.
For information, please contact ASQ Quality Press at 800-248-1946, or write to
ASQ Quality Press, P.O. Box 3005, Milwaukee, WI 53201-3005.

To place orders or to request a free copy of the ASQ Quality Press Publications
Catalog, including ASQ membership information, call 800-248-1946. Visit our
Web site at www.asq.org or http://qualitypress.asq.org .

Printed in the United States of America

 Printed on acid-free paper

Contents

Introduction

This book focuses on methods and techniques to conduct process audits. Internal and external process audits provide very valuable information to management and oversight organizations. Though *process audit* is defined in several texts, there is no book or standard of common conventions or accepted practices.

In this book we will follow along the sequence of the diagram on page xi (see Figure I.1) with each step corresponding to a chapter. Every attempt has been made to focus on process audit techniques and to not repeat common system audit practices found in books such as *The Quality Audit Handbook*. Readers of *The Process Auditing Techniques Guide* should already know basic auditing techniques, such as how to conduct interviews or develop a checklist. The techniques presented in this book can be used by auditors who conduct first-, second-, and third-party audits to any standard or work instruction. For convenience, ANSI/ISO/ASQ Q9001-2000 examples are used in the book, but other controls and standards such as FAA, FDA, EPA, OHSA could be used also.

A chapter on auditing to ANSI/ISO/ASQ Q9001-2000 has been included because of the standard style changes and quality management system design. The ANSI/ISO/ASQ Q9001-2000 quality management system design should be based on defining, linking, sequencing and measuring processes. Where applicable, process audit techniques can be used to evaluate the quality management system.

1 **Understand Process Principles**
Process inputs, transformation, outputs,
PEEMMM elements, control,
feedback loop, system

↓

2 **Prepare for the Audit**
Process audit strategy, purpose, scope, team,
audit plan, contact, steps on PFD,
tree diagram, checklist

↓

3 **Start the Audit**
Opening meeting, tour to collect numbers,
data collection plans, team meetings

↓

4 **Use Process Audit Techniques**
Tracing, PEEMMM, output objectives, adequacy
of control, risk, error proofing, optimization,
PDCA, ACDP, open-ended requirements

↓

5 **Auditing to ANSI/ISO/ASQ Q9001-2000**
Need for new techniques, strategic and
tactical changes

↓

6 **Analyze and Report Findings**
Compliance, adequate, meets
objectives, performance, risks, optimal,
robustness, report

Figure I.1 Process auditing detailed steps.

Chapter 1

Understand Process Principles

In order to audit a process, you must first understand what it is. With my background in chemical engineering and business management, I am very familiar with processes. Chemical engineering could more appropriately be called process engineering. The very first engineering class that I took was called *Process Principles*. It was considered a difficult class and the demands of the class caused many students to explore alternate career paths. In this beginner class, the students were taught about designing processes, determining duties to be performed, establishing specifications and requirements, and integrating the various units (activities) into a coordinated plan. Additionally, we were told that "problems cannot be segregated and each treated individually without consideration of the others."[1] So the first principle we learned was that process activities are connected or linked. Secondly, we learned that processes are responsible for the changes that take place within a system. Some call this change a *transformation*.

1

The balancing and equilibrium of inputs and outputs is called the *Law of Conservation.* The Law of Conservation requires that the sum of the inputs equal the sum of the outputs for a given process. For example, the uncut metal plate input equals the fabricated bracket, plus scrap and metal filings.

The third principle is that the Law of Conservation applies to a defined process. For processes to work, inputs and outputs must be in balance. If process elements are out of balance, the objectives would not be achieved and the process would not be effective. The output objective demands certain inputs and if you don't have sufficient inputs, the outputs will never be achieved.

A fourth principle is that processes can be operated at a set of optimum conditions for best utilization of resources and achievement of objectives. Economics is an important consideration of design and process operation. Every process has a set of optimum operating conditions for achieving both economic and performance objectives.

Process Principles	
1	Activities are linked as sequential steps.
2	Change (transformation) takes place.
3	The Law of Conservation applies to a defined process.
4	Optimization results in best utilization of resources.

Process Description

A process transforms inputs into outputs. This transformation or change takes place as a series of activities or steps that lead to a desired result (objective). The *process approach* way of doing things is more effective in achieving objectives than a haphazard or random approach. Establishing a process is good, but it could be either a good process or a bad process—similar to the thought captured in the saying "A bad plan is better than no plan."

Inputs can be tangible or intangible. Inputs may come in the form of people, equipment, materials, parts, assemblies, components, information, money, and so on (see Figure 1.1). The process transforms, changes, or converts the inputs into an output. Inputs are the thing(s) that will be transformed and the transformation mechanisms.

An output may be a product or service. Outputs can include: parts, assemblies, materials, information, energy, money, machines, devices, completed

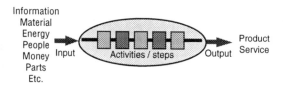

Figure 1.1 Process inputs.

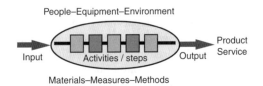

Figure 1.2 Process equilibrium.

treatment, performance of a skill, and so on. The output product is a result of the process.

There are many other inputs to a process (other than the object of the transformation) that make it possible to complete the transformation. It is convenient to categorize these as *process elements*. The process elements can be divided into six groups that contain all the factors that make up a process. The six groups are people, equipment, environment, materials, measures, and methods (PEEMMM)(see Figure 1.2). If the process is making a peanut butter and jelly sandwich, we will be transforming the materials of peanut butter, jelly, and bread into a sandwich.

Example: Sandwich Making Process

People–Equipment–Environment–Materials–Measures–Methods

Question	Answer	Explanation
Are people involved in this process?	Yes	We need a chef.

Continued

Continued

Do we need equipment to complete this process?	Yes	A knife to spread the ingredients and perhaps a cutting board.
Are there any environmental considerations?	Yes	The area needs to be clean. There should not be any water on the cutting board or counter top that the bread might soak up.
Are materials needed?	Yes	Grape jelly, bread, and crunchy peanut butter.
Are there measures or standards?	Yes	We need to ensure that the sandwich consumer is pleased with the outcome.
Do we need a method?	Yes	We will need a recipe that will tell the steps, order, and amounts.

In a machine shop, there may be a process for making brackets that transforms a metal plate into H brackets. The inputs of the process may include the following:

Example: H Bracket Stamping Process

People–Equipment–Environment–Materials–Measures–Methods

Question	Answer	Explanation
Are people involved in this process?	Yes	Machine operator, material helper
Do we need equipment to complete this process?	Yes	250 ton stamping machine, tote bin, scrap cart, tags, safety equipment

Continued

Continued

Are there any environmental considerations?	Yes	Housekeeping (look for excessive dust, no oil on floor)
Are materials needed?	Yes	Machine oil, cut and sized metal plate
Are there measures or standards?	Yes	Check dimensions with calipers per traveler
Do we need a method?	Yes	Traveler (work order), work instruction 075-H-02, safety manual

In all cases, there must be sufficient inputs to achieve the output. There must be a balance or equilibrium between inputs and outputs (Law of Conservation). For example, if you want to make 1000 H brackets, there has to be the required amount of metal, energy, and machine time. If inputs are too few, too many, or different from the process needs, the process will be suboptimal.[2] Too few inputs will result in a shortfall; too many will result in excessive waste; and anything other than the required inputs will result in an ineffective process and/or chaos.

Control of Processes

In most cases, it is desirable to control processes to avoid negative consequences. The amount or level of control varies depending on the risk and acceptability of undesirable outcomes. The severity or level of control for nuclear plant processes will be different from that of any organization that publishes a magazine or newspaper. The essential requirement for any control system is that there is a feedback information loop (see Figure 1.3) from the process output. The feedback information is used to adjust the process or make decisions about the output (before the next process or before the customer receives it). Feedback information may be in the form of temperature, pressure, dimension, weight, volume, count, color, condition, or portion. The function of the control feedback loop is to achieve output targets and objectives.

For management to control a process or activity, it must establish a predetermined method. Without it, there is no basis to adjust or improve the process. Predetermined methods can include: plans, procedures, work instructions, checklists, outlines, diagrams, flowcharts, step-by-step software program codes, process maps, and so on.

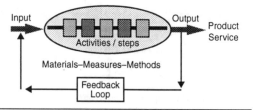

Figure 1.3 Process feedback loop.

Feedback information should relate to the process performance criteria and/or objectives. Feedback can be in the form of a quality characteristic such as activity level or dimensions, and feedback can be a performance measure such as yield, cost, waste, delays, utilization, error rate, field failures, satisfaction, and so on. Sometimes it is easier to monitor a process parameter such as temperature or pressure that is a function or indicator of the performance of the process. For example, we can monitor the temperature of a process because we know that if it goes above 107 degrees centigrade, the product will darken and fail the color test. Without a feedback, loop objectives cannot be assured.

For example, there may be a process that transforms sheet metal into an H bracket with specified holes for fasteners (see Figure 1.4). One of the most critical parameters may be the diameter of the holes.

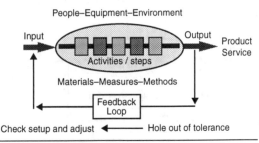

Figure 1.4 H bracket process control.

For this process, the feedback loop is the diameter of the holes. This information can be used to reject parts or make adjustments to the fabrication process (machine, drill bits, and so on).

In some cases, you may want to use statistical techniques to better understand what changes need to be made to the process to ensure that output objectives are achieved. For example, statistical process control (SPC) charts may be used to monitor a process variable to ensure that the process is capable and out-of-control points are acted upon.

Processes Make the System

Processes must be organized with other processes to achieve objectives, such as manufacturing and distributing parts for a profit. Processes are sequenced and linked to achieve certain business/organization objectives (see Figure 1.5). An organization can be

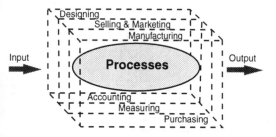

Figure 1.5 Product organization.

considered a collection of processes, all of which are working together to transform inputs into outputs.

The combination of product/service processes with management processes creates a system. Processes can be simple or complex, similar or dissimilar. The system brings the processes together for a common purpose that may relate to business, services, quality, environment, or safety.

The ANSI/ISO/ASQ Q9001-2000 standard is organized as a set of quality management system processes and it requires organizations to use a *process approach* for managing and operating the QMS (see Figure 1.6). The process approach is basically

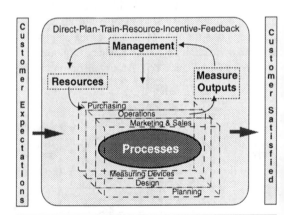

Figure 1.6   Business system model.

sequencing and controlling transformations to achieve common objectives. The process approach is a more effective way of managing and hence organizations will benefit by using it.

Advanced Process and System Modeling

There are other palatable modeling techniques. Appendix A has information about what is called the IDEF3 Process Flow and Objective State Description Capture Method Overview. IDEF stands for Integrated DEFinition. The IDEF methodology may be used to model a wide variety of automated and nonautomated systems or subject areas, including any combination of hardware, software, machines, processes, or people. The IDEF modeling techniques can be used to model very complex systems and processes. This model uses the term mechanisms to describe the people and machines that do the transformation work. If you are interested in sources of additional information, review references in Appendix A.

Summary

When using process techniques to audit processes and management systems, you need to remember process fundamentals. Processes are characterized by certain principles. Visual models (such as the ones used in this chapter) can describe processes and their elements and control. The principles and models will help you analyze processes to determine their strengths and weaknesses.

In chapter 2, we will get organized for an audit and learn how auditing processes and process techniques are different from and more powerful than other audit methods.

Chapter 2

Prepare for the Audit

In this chapter we will discuss the steps for preparing for a process audit. We assume you already know auditing basics; therefore we will not elaborate on the basics that are common to all types of audits. If you are not familiar with the auditing process, you should consider taking an Internal Auditing Basics class. We are following the steps below as we proceed from chapter to chapter.

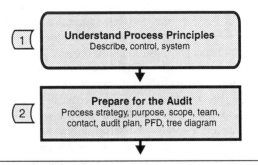

Process auditing steps 1 and 2.

SECTION I: ORGANIZING THE AUDIT

Process Auditing

By virtue of its name, a *process audit* is an audit of a process against agreed-upon requirements. A process audit is used to verify that processes are operating within specified limits and achieving specified targets (objectives). A *process quality audit* examines an activity to verify that inputs, actions, and outputs are in accordance with defined requirements.[4] A process audit is an evaluation of the sequential steps and interactions of a process within a system. The *process* term is also used to describe techniques used when conducting an audit. For example, an auditor may use process audit techniques during a management system audit.

By its very nature, process auditing implies an action such as transforming inputs into outputs. Dennis Arter (author of *Quality Audits for Improved Performance*) has always linked process auditing to an action verb such as filling, stamping, purchasing, reacting, cutting, and so on. Process auditing is evaluating the steps and activities that create the action or transform the inputs into outputs. This is a very useful approach because it focuses on the work cycle and deliverables instead of on isolated requirements.

Many standards are organized in a random series of elements or sections. This results in auditors auditing organizations element by element to verify conformance to requirements. This is sometimes called the *element method.* Auditing by element is a very effective method for tracing requirements but does not consider the inputs, outputs, and interacting activities of other processes and therefore is less effective overall.

One example of a drawback of the element method is that an auditor may be assigned the calibration control element (clause 7.6) to audit. It would be easy for the auditor to go to the quality assurance department (see Figure 2.1) without regard to the devices used in manufacturing or in engineering. Also, using the element method, manufacturing (see Figure 2.1) may not be audited for

		Purch.	Mfg.	Eng.	Sales	QA
7.2	Customer				░	
7.3	Design			░		
7.4	Purchasing	░				
7.5.1	Production		░			
7.5.2	Validation					░
7.5.3	Id & Trace.		░			
7.5.4	Cust. Prop.					░
7.5.5	Pres. Prod.		░			
7.6	Devices					░
8.1	Planning					░
8.2	Customer Sat.				░	

Figure 2.1 Audit strategy: Element method schedule.

inputs of customer requirements or engineering changes. Another example of element method weakness is not linking the purchasing department's responsibility to monitor supplier performance with QA's incoming inspection results during the audit. It is common for one auditor to be assigned purchasing while another auditor is assigned receiving and inspection, resulting in the linkages and common processes between the two areas going untested.

Process auditing provides value by evaluating processes, their controls, risks, and the achievement of objectives. Auditors and management can benefit by conducting process audits and using process techniques to better test and evaluate system controls.

Purpose and Scope

One of the main differences between a process and system audit is scope definition and expansion. A process audit could be a singular process or part of a process such as filling, washing, reacting, drilling, cutting, treating, transporting, informing, ordering, and so on. Process audits can start at any level that work takes place. If we refer to the control levels triangle (see Figure 2.2), we can see that process audits can start from level 4 and go up to the top, while system audits start from the top (level 1) and go down. A system audit is an audit of a system (or subsystem) against agreed-upon requirements.

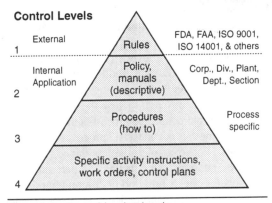

Figure 2.2 Control levels triangle.

Top-level requirements drive the formation of sub-systems and processes to meet requirements.

The control levels triangle (see Figure 2.2) illustrates the hierarchal nature of management tools (standards, procedures, instructions, plans, and so on) used to describe (specify) a process (what it is supposed to look like). Typically, organizations are audited against the predetermined process requirements listed in the controls triangle.

At the bottom (simplest) level of the triangle, the scope of a process audit can be a single activity (transformation) described by a work instruction, procedure, or other means to predetermine the process steps. The process audit may be conducted to:

(1) monitor the effectiveness and efficiency of the activity or (2) verify conformance to requirements. Process audits may also be used to troubleshoot problem processes. At level 4 (see Figure 2.2), it is very easy to follow and audit a given path or process steps. As you move up the triangle, it becomes more difficult to test the process flow because the interconnected processes may be run at different times or locations, and process complexity increases. For example, the combined drilling, forming, stamping, and finishing of a part may take place over a week's time and in different buildings. Many process materials are done in batches or held in tanks waiting on the next treatment. Hospital services for admitting, informing, treating, medicating, and discharging patients do not take place at the same time. At the management system level (quality, environment, safety, business), the idea of a process audit becomes obscure because of the multiple processes within processes with differing constraints and objectives. As we break down a system into subsystems and functions, we begin to see distinct processes (purchasing, ordering, forming, recording, and filling) that transform inputs into outputs to meet specified goals.

Third-, second-, and first-party auditors may conduct process audits. Third-party auditors may verify that certain licensed or certified processes are in compliance with regulations and contracts such as welding, grading, incubating, pressure vessel testing, or aircraft engine repair. For second-party audits, auditors may conduct a process audit to verify a specified method, practice, or procedure as part of a contract or purchased service. For example, you may outsource or hire an organization to perform a specified task, such as inspecting your fire extinguishers, building molds, storage of hazardous waste, or calibration of equipment. As a control, you could conduct a process audit of a service to verify that agreed-upon requirements are being met and the process is effective. Internal process audits can be very beneficial because they can be used to verify controls, identify weaknesses that can be eliminated, and identify causes of problems.

There may be many reasons for conducting a process audit or only one. The following are some reasons to conduct a process audit, which are also examples of process audit purpose statements:

- Determine if established practices (procedure, work instruction, policy) are being effectively implemented and maintained.

- Determine if the process conforms to international standards.

- Assess effectiveness and identify opportunities for improvement.

- Verify controls are adequate and identify organization risks.
- Identify potential root causes of a stated problem.
- Verify that contractual (certification, license) requirements are being maintained for a specific activity or process.
- Verify that corrective action plans were implemented and are meeting objectives.

The scope of a process audit can be very simple, or very complex and technical. Any process can be audited, but normally processes are audited because of external requirements, level of risk, or importance to the organization.

Example process audit scopes:

- Operating (machines or equipment)
- Tracing the flow of information or paper trail
- Performing a repair or technique
- Flowcharting a method or procedure
- Transacting
- Grading, marking, or inspecting
- Treating or performing
- Manufacturing or servicing

- Packaging, labeling, and storing
- Finishing or preparing
- Screening or evaluating

The audit client or audit sponsor determines the process audit purpose and scope.

Audit Team

Most audits are done by a single auditor auditing a single activity (level 4). That auditor should be knowledgeable in process auditing and the process being audited. Knowledge of the process may come from a combination of industry experience and first-hand knowledge of the process under review.

In some cases, process audit teams are formed. If you needed to audit several discrete processes at the same time, you would need several auditors with the appropriate experience to audit the processes. The following are examples of when several auditors would be needed:

- The second- or third-party audit organization may need to check x-ray, drug testing, die check, and stress testing during one visit.

- There is a need to form a team so that sampling (interviewing) could take place at the same time because it is the only way to collect accurate data.

- There may be special circumstances (such as suspected wrongdoing).

- There will be more than one auditor to save on on-site audit time (minimize disruptions).

An example of the latter is that a team of auditors could conduct a packing area (see Figure 2.3) process audit. One team member could monitor the action steps, another could monitor the instrument use and its maintenance, and a third may check administrative records, such as determination of competency and completion of training.

As we move up (levels 3 and 2) to auditing groups of connected processes or an entire function, it may be necessary to increase the audit time or size of the audit team. For example, a process audit of the

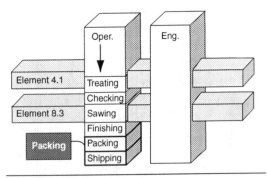

Figure 2.3 Auditing strategies: Department/Function/Area/Strategies.

operations group may require several auditors to cover all the activities (ordering, scheduling, routing, reacting, finishing, packing, and storing). In the airline industry, process audits are used to verify controls for aircraft engine repair, in-flight operations, compliance with safety requirements, and so on.

The number of people on the team is proportional to the scope, purpose, and time allocated to the audit. Every process audit should have a lead auditor. This person is responsible for coordinating the audit with the auditee, ensuring the audit team is prepared, and managing the performance of the audit (service).

Contacting the Auditee

The protocol for contacting the auditee for a process audit is no different from any other audit. However, the information you want is different.

For a process audit of a baseline process (level 4), you may want the following information:

- Work instructions or procedures
- Plans, control plans
- Process description by flowchart or other means
- Key characteristics and check points in the process
- Acceptance criteria and/or objectives

- Identified bottlenecks (the capacity or output limiting step)

- Constraints (market demand, storage space, labor)

- Process control charts or other statistical analysis

- Product and service inputs

- Product and service outputs

Not all the information you want may be available, but that in itself will be valuable information. For example, if the process bottleneck is not known, it probably means the process is operating suboptimally. If a process is operating at capacity, the bottleneck is probably known. If the process is at or near capacity and the bottleneck is not known, then you have already identified an area for improvement.

If our process audit scope is the operations function, you need the same process information, only it should be at the corresponding level. Instead of detailed work instructions you will want the area procedures or policies. Instead of a packing area flowchart, you will want to see the operations area process steps from open order to filled order. In your mind, draw a circle around the area to be audited and seek information relative to your scope (see Figure 2.4).

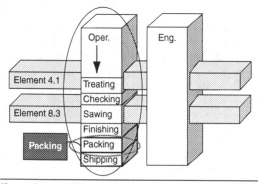

Figure 2.4 Auditing strategies:
Department/Function/Area/Strategies.

In our example, you may be doing a detailed process audit of the packing area or a process audit of operations. Before ending this phase of the audit, be sure to confirm all the audit information, so everyone is in agreement with the purpose, scope, time, and so on.

Next we will look at how to prepare for a process audit. We will need to learn how to use different techniques to ensure success.

SECTION II: PROCESS AUDIT PREPARATION ACTIVITIES

The preparation activities for a process audit are the same as for any audit, except it is geared to collecting information about the process inputs, transformations, interactions, and outputs.

Audit Plan

Audit plans will vary depending on the audit purpose, scope, and whether it is an internal or external audit. The lead auditor normally prepares the audit plan. For a process audit of an activity or area, you should consider the following as part of the audit plan:

Audit purpose/objective:

Determine if the process has been effectively implemented and maintained. Recall the audit purposes discussed earlier in this chapter.

Audit scope:

The area or activity should be clearly identified. It should be clear that any input or output of the process under examination is considered to be part of the scope. There are no firewalls when it comes to process auditing. In fact, testing the connectivity and process flow is a requirement.

Audit criteria:

Auditors always audit against an agreed-upon criteria. The criteria must be documented in some manner, such as in work instructions or objectives. For a process audit, it will be the process procedures, methods, plans, and work instructions. A process could also be audited for adherence to organization policy or documented goals, such as quality objectives. For an audit of a single process activity (level 4), the audit criteria may be a work instruction (such

---

as packing instructions). For an audit of a surgical procedure, the audit criteria may be administrative procedures, standard practices, and training materials. For a process audit of an area (with many processes), we need to step back and look at all processes within that area or function. For example, in purchasing we may look at the process of selecting, approving, purchasing, monitoring, and retaining suppliers.

The audit criteria will also include any applicable laws, regulations, external standards such as ANSI/ISO/ASQ Q9001 or ANSI/ISO 14001, organization policy, and internal standards, such as procedures or work instructions.

Logistics (date, time, duration, resources):

For external audits, several process audits may be scheduled at one time period (1 to 3 days) to conserve expenses. For internal audits, process audits can be one hour to one day. If an organization conducted a particular process audit over several shifts, it may be important to schedule an audit for every shift to identify any differences (weaknesses and strengths of each). If process audits are being used to follow up a corrective action, it may be necessary to schedule several audits over time to ensure the corrective action is sustained.

If the audit team has any special resource needs, such as office space or equipment, such needs should be handled as they would in any audit.

Audit team members:

The lead auditor assigns an area of responsibility for each team member and identifies any specialists that have been asked to accompany the team. If there are several members on the audit team, it is helpful to list their expertise area, such as calibration, engines, tooling, medical, molds, control, repair, training, and so on.

Be sure to get the plan approved by the client or representative of the area to be audited. There should also be agreement on what type of information will be included in the audit report. For process audits, keep reporting as simple as possible.

Process Flow Diagramming for the Audit

The primary tool of process auditing is the process flow diagram (PFD) or flowchart. Charting the process steps (sequential activities) is an effective method for describing the process. For auditing purposes, process flow diagrams should be used to identify sequential process steps (activities) and kept as simple or as reasonable as possible.

Follow along the method shown in Figure 2.5 for creating a process flow diagram. The PFD work instruction is organized by key word, step description, inputs, who is responsible, and a visual reference.

Steps	Description	Inputs (PEEMMM)	Who?	Picture
1- Start	Arrange meeting (if an audit team) and collect materials for flowcharting the process to be audited.	+ Procedure + Existing PFD + Paper, flipchart, or software + Charting method	Lead auditor	
2- Determine purpose and level	State purpose and how detailed the PFD should be. The PFD purpose should support the auditor, the audit purpose, and scope.	+ Audit Plan + Suitable location: office, conference room + Subject matter expert (SME)	Lead auditor and audit team	
3- Determine starting and ending point	Determine where the process starts. The need may be created by an order, schedule, request, or inquiry.	+ Materials collected in step 1 + Subject matter expert (SME)	Lead auditor and audit team	
4- Trace from beginning to end	Trace the process steps (activities) and determine the inputs and outputs of each step. Diagram it from an existing procedure or chart, or expert knowledge.	+ Materials collected in step 1 + Subject matter expert (SME)	Lead auditor and audit team	

Figure 2.5 Creating a PFD for the audit.

Continued

Continued

5- Add key audit information ↓	Add test, checkpoints, or inspection. Add people responsible for the step or activity. Add procedure, standard, or contract references. Add records and form number. These are important points that can be verified during the audit.	+ Materials collected in step 1 + Subject matter expert (SME) + Appropriate standard or document + Blank or example records	Lead auditor or audit team	
6- Looks good? ↓	Title the PFD and check for completeness and accuracy (inputs, outputs, closed loops). If not okay, modify and recheck.	+ Legible + Complete + Accurate	Lead auditor and audit team	
7- Publish the PFD	Ensure the PFD will be available to the audit team.	+ Reproduction equipment and software + Appropriate medium + Legible	Lead auditor and audit team	Report

Figure 2.5   Creating a PFD for the audit.

Using Software?

Software can make flowcharting easier. By using software, it is possible to flowchart a procedure or work instruction as you are reading it. Some software programs allow you to enter text and code it (as a statement, decision, or multiple choices) as you are typing. When you are finished reading the document and entering your key words, the software will automatically flowchart it for you. However, unless you are proficient in the use of the flowchart software, it is best to keep things simple. It is too easy to be pulled into figuring out how to use all the software features and lose sight of the job (preparing for the audit).

In our Parts PFD example (see Figure 2.6), each step shows who performs the work and the procedure number. You can also color-code the actions or the different departments that are involved in the process to ensure it meets parts fabrication objectives. If you count maintenance, four department activities must be coordinated for the process to operate at optimal conditions. For the sake of brevity, we have marked flows as accept-reject or approved-not approved, instead of a separate decision step using the diamond decision symbol convention (see Appendix E for standard flowchart symbols).

The PFD provides a clear audit trail from the beginning of the run to the end. It also shows the interaction of other processes. Flowcharting is a

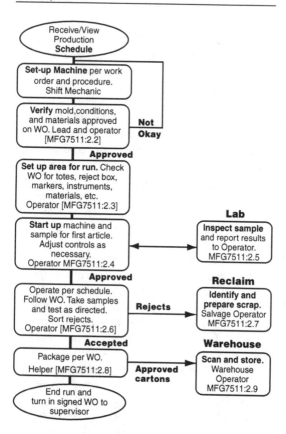

Figure 2.6 PFD for manufacturing parts.

very effective method for evaluating processes and providing fact-based (ANSI/ISO/ASQ Q9001-2000 Quality Management Principle #7) information for management decisions.

In general, the PFD should be at the same level as the scope of the process audit. The parts flowchart could be used to conduct a process audit of the manufacturing line. If the scope were to evaluate the reclaim operation, there would be a flowchart of just the reclaim steps.

It is okay to share your PFD with the auditee. If there is no existing PFD, the auditee may use your diagram for training or FMEA (failure mode and effects analysis) evaluations.

In addition to creating a PFD, you should tour the area before you start interviewing. You will learn the common names of things and activities. You will also be able to write down the lot, project, part, and batch number of products or services being processed at the time.

Another diagramming or charting technique is *process mapping*. The complexity of process maps can vary, but for auditing, simplicity is the key. In Appendix F you can view an example process map of a packing operation. The process flow may not be as straight forward using a process map compared to a PFD, but area responsibilities are much easier to see and understand.

Now that you know the process, you will need to check actual performance to the agreed-upon criteria. Normally, requirements are listed on a checklist and checked off as each requirement is verified. Although checklists are very good tools, a tree diagram may be more useful for a process audit.

Tree Diagrams

For process audits, *tree diagrams* showing process elements and controls are more useful than the standard checklist. Typically we divide the process elements into the same groupings we discussed earlier (PEEMMM). The six groups represent the inputs to a process for controlling and transforming. A tree diagram will help guide you during the interviewing of the people operating the process. A generic version may look like Figure 2.7.

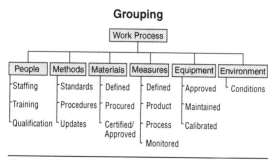

Figure 2.7 Tree diagram for a process.

While auditing, questions such as the following may be derived from the process tree diagram:

- People
  1. Were you trained to do this job?
  2. How were you qualified or certified?
  3. What do you do to stay qualified?

- Equipment
  1. What equipment do you need?
  2. How is it maintained?
  3. How do you know it is okay to use?

- Environment
  1. Are there any special environmental conditions (temperature, lighting, or housekeeping) for operating the process?
  2. Are there any workstation requirements (safety, ergonomics) for performing the job?

- Materials
  1. What materials do you use?
  2. How do you know they are okay to use?
  3. What do you do with bad materials?

- Measures
  1. How do you know the process is operating as needed?

   2. Do you check the output?
   3. What do you check it against?

- Methods
  1. How do you know what to do?
  2. Do you have access to procedures, flowcharts, work instructions, and so on? Show me.
  3. How do you know it is kept up-to-date?

Continuing on with the tree diagram, we can add references to specified controls in a standard. ANSI/ISO/ASQ Q9001-2000 is referenced in the tree diagram for manufacturing run (see Figure 2.8), but you can reference any appropriate standard, such as ANSI/ISO 14001 or ISO/TS 16949. You can use the tree diagram for manufacturing run as an example for developing your own, using appropriate standards depending on your type of organization.

We can easily refer to our tree diagram during the audit to ask questions and test the controls of the process. We can also see the overlap between functions and performance standard requirements.

Another use of the tree diagram is to summarize the controls to be tested by clause. It is like a quick view of a checklist that has all the required controls listed by key word. For example, if we were going

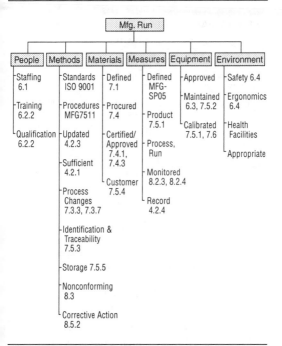

Figure 2.8 Tree diagram for manufacturing run.

to conduct an audit of the purchasing area we could organize the clause requirements in a tree diagram. The tree diagram by clause (see Figure 2.9) could be used with a checklist during a system audit.

ANSI/ISO/ASQ Q9001 Quality System Standard

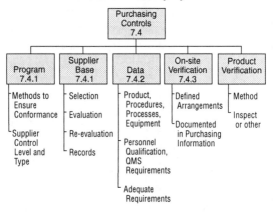

Figure 2.9 Tree diagram by clause.

Tree diagrams can be applied to a wide range of different activities and facilities (construction, maintenance, healthcare, airline, operations). You will spend less time developing questions and more time understanding the process. The tree diagrams are also excellent communication tools when interfacing with the auditee. You can show the auditee the areas you are interested in.

Checklist

You should already know how to construct a good checklist and we will not take the time to review it here. However, the role of the checklist in a process audit is different from that in a system audit.

For an internal audit, a checklist may be something you reference after observing and interviewing. You may want to reference the checklist periodically to ensure all requirements were examined. If you are auditing a machine setup process or reclaim process, you may not have any external standard (such as ANSI/ISO/ASQ Q9001) checklist questions. You may only have questions taken from the setup or reclaim procedure (if one exists). Remember, for a process audit, the objective is to test the controls of the process.

For a second-party audit, a checklist will be a handy reference against either contract or national or international standard requirements. But even so, you should be evaluating the process inputs and outputs during the process audit to verify that they meet objectives. Following a checklist will actually slow you down unless you reorganize (reorder) the checklist in the same way as the process is organized or sequenced.

Third-party auditors normally use a checklist referencing the requirement for product, process, and system audits. Auditors conducting third-party management system audits don't normally have time to do process audits. However, they can use process auditing techniques to support the process approach. Later (in chapter 4), we will talk about how to use process techniques to audit functions and departments within a management system.

In chapter 3, we will take the tools we have learned about and use them to perform a process audit. Process audits are powerful because they are an independent means to verify that the process is working as intended.

Chapter 3

Start the Audit

The same basic audit performance conventions are followed for a process audit as for a system audit. We will briefly review those steps here and note any differences or change in emphasis between the two types of audits. The opening meeting is the start of the performance phase of the audit.

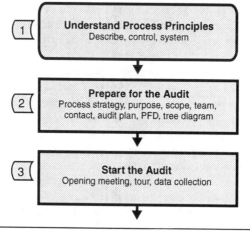

1. **Understand Process Principles**
Describe, control, system

2. **Prepare for the Audit**
Process strategy, purpose, scope, team, contact, audit plan, PFD, tree diagram

3. **Start the Audit**
Opening meeting, tour, data collection

Process auditing steps 1–3.

Opening Meeting

Most process audits are done by one auditor, who is also the lead auditor. If there is more than one auditor, all the auditors should attend the opening meeting. For a *simple internal process audit*, the opening meeting may be in the supervisor's office and the auditee may be represented by a senior technician or first-line supervisor. For a more *complex process audit* (a team of auditors examining different processes) or external process audits, the opening meeting will be more formal and there may be several auditee representatives from the different processes to be audited. The lead auditor is responsible for arranging and organizing the opening meeting.

Even if you have done this same audit several times before and everyone knows you're the internal process auditor, there should still be an opening meeting. If the internal audit plan calls for multiple audits of the same process, one opening meeting may be sufficient to cover multiple audits in the plan. Multiple audits of the same process may be scheduled to check different shifts, different operators, or the same operator performing the same process at different times. However, even if it is a routine audit, you must always let management acknowledge that you are in the area.

The standard opening meeting conventions should be followed. Normally, simple internal process audit opening meetings are very short unless it is the first time. The agenda for a simple routine internal process audit opening meeting may be:

- Greetings.

- Are there any *change*s or concerns about the audit plan?

- Are there any *safety* or other restrictions?

- Is there anything we *should know about*, such as a test, trial run or customer visit?

- Is everyone *available* to be interviewed?

- Thanks, let's get started.

For a first time internal process audit or an external process audit, consider the following agenda items for the opening meeting:

- *Complete introductions.* Make sure everyone knows each other. This is an ideal time to take attendance (check off a list or pass around a sign-in sheet).

- *Thank your host.* Thank the person (or acknowledge him or her) who made the arrangements for the audit. This can be anyone who coordinated the audit.

- *Review the audit plan.* Reaffirm the purpose, scope, and performance standards to be audited against (chapter 2). If corrective actions from prior audits are to be verified as part of the audit, this should be in the purpose, too. You should clarify any unclear details of the audit plan.

- *Limited access.* Any accessibility limitations placed on the auditors should have been identified prior to the opening meeting, but be prepared to address any last minute issues. The auditor's access to certain areas may be limited for several reasons. Follow standard practices for addressing confidentiality issues.

Figure 3.1 Access limited.

- *Explain your methods and techniques.*
  Explain how data will be collected, such as
  observing activities, interviewing operators,
  and/or checking records and instructions.
  Since process audits are very closely aligned
  with individual performance, it is important
  to emphasize the process focus of checking
  the inputs and outputs against objectives of
  the process. At times, process audits can
  appear to be auditing individual performance
  and make interviewees nervous.

- *Explain the reporting process.* Explain how
  the data collected during the investigation
  will be reported and followed-up. The results
  of an audit may be reported as finding
  statements, nonconformities, and
  improvement points. Explain how the
  relative importance of results is categorized,
  such as major and minor findings or rated as
  high, medium, or low risk.

- *Pass out the interview schedule* (for complex
  process and external audits). Most process
  audits don't need an interview schedule
  because auditors go to the process area and
  start interviewing the people responsible for
  the process. If it is a complex process that
  has several steps, it may be necessary to

issue a schedule of where the auditor(s) will be each hour of the audit. Confirm the availability of personnel (interviewees and escorts) and *resolve interview schedule conflicts*.

- *Review logistics* (for complex process and external audits). Review working hours, arrangements for escorts, and means and time to travel to and from the process area. For external audits, you should verify meeting room locations, home base for the auditors, and necessary equipment and services (electrical power outlets, restrooms, telephones). *Verify arrangements* for lunch and break times.

- *Confirm exit meeting.* For internal process audits, you can either schedule the exit meeting immediately after the audit or in the next day or two. However, if the time between the performance of the audit and exit meeting is excessive, it can reduce the effectiveness of the audit.

As with all audits, keep a record of attendance and a record of any changes to the audit plan, schedule, and actions items requiring follow-up.

You may share your tree diagram and PFD with the auditee. Do not be surprised if, after reviewing your PFD, the auditee points to a process step and says, "We don't do that anymore." Then you need to find out how it works now and why it is different from what you expected.

Tour

For complex or external process audits, a post-opening meeting tour is a good technique to become familiar with the layout, identify changes since the last audit, and align what you see with your expectations (the PFD). Tours should be brief. During the tour you should start recording numbers and observations. You should record batch, lot, part, traveler, customer identification number, routing card, form, transaction, room number, and order numbers. When doing a system audit or complex process audit, the auditor must have a means to connect the different processes. Knowing what is being processed, readied to ship, or what the new inputs are will be very useful.

Touring

* Current
* Traceable
* Accurate

Before recording the numbers, verify that they are traceable for your purposes. For example, you may have recorded several part numbers only to find out later that orders can only be traced by work order number.

Take time to ensure the accuracy of the numbers. Missing numbers, transpositions, and illegible numbers will cause you problems later on.

You can also get your numbers from daily shipping reports, customer order sheets, service and manufacturing schedules, current or closed project lists, and so on. Whether you are conducting a process or system audit, you should find a method to acquire the data you need to trace the product or service.

Other Meetings During the Audit

For simple internal process audits, the only meetings are the opening and closing meetings. For complex or external process audits, it may be necessary to hold audit team meetings and auditee daily briefings. Meetings should be as brief as possible, in that meeting time is not audit time. Typical meeting agendas are:

Audit team meeting agenda	Auditee daily briefing agenda
• Share data/evidence/ information • Re-plan assignments • Review and record observations • Determine conformance • Start the reporting process	• Verify processes completed • Confirm processes to be completed tomorrow • Identify problems uncovered

Data Collection Plans

The sources of data in a process audit are no different from a system audit. Sources of data include: records, documents, interviews, analysis, observations, and physical data (see Figure 3.2).

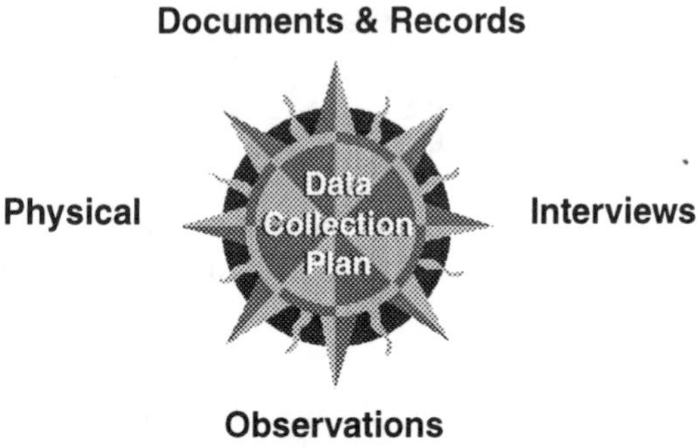

Documents & Records

Physical   **Interviews**

Observations

Figure 3.2   Data collection plan.

The PFD is the key to your data collection plan. It will show the documents and records you want to see. The PFD also shows the tangible inputs and outputs that you can verify during interviews and observations.

Now that you are ready to start auditing, in chapter 4 we will discuss process techniques that can be used to test controls even if there are no procedures or specific requirements.

Chapter 4

Use Process Audit Techniques

SECTION I: INVESTIGATING (COLLECTING EVIDENCE)

Armed with your knowledge of the process (based on your preparation), you are ready to evaluate the process. Depending on the audit purpose, you will need to collect evidence to:

- Verify the process conforms to standards and internal methods.

- Ensure objectives are being achieved.

- Ensure controls are adequate and risks are acceptable.

- Identify areas for improvement.

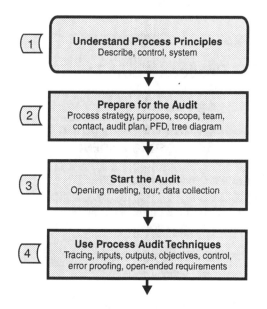

Process auditing steps 1–4.

Tracing

The primary strategy for conducting a process audit is to trace the process steps from activity to activity (sequence and interaction). *Tracing* is used to follow the path of a process to test out controls. You can trace forward or backward. As you trace you should ask questions about *People, Equipment, Environment, Materials, Measures, and Methods.*

The PFD helps you follow along the path and identifies process owners that need to be interviewed and check points that need to be explored. The tree diagram helps auditors ask the right questions for identification of weaknesses.

The tracing sample taking and testing (see Figure 4.1) may help you formulate interview questions as you trace through the process. You should also refer to your process tree diagram to help you formulate questions such as:

- What kind of training did you receive?

- Is there a procedure for taking samples? Where is it?

- What containers do you use for the sample? Who approves them?

- How do you know when to take a sample? Do you keep a record?

- How do you know how much of a sample to take?

- Is the sampling device approved?

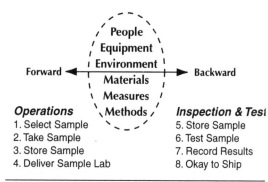

Forward ◄─────────────► **Backward**

People
Equipment
Environment
Materials
Measures
Methods

Operations
1. Select Sample
2. Take Sample
3. Store Sample
4. Deliver Sample Lab

Inspection & Test
5. Store Sample
6. Test Sample
7. Record Results
8. Okay to Ship

Figure 4.1 Tracing sample taking and testing.

The following are some example interview questions you may ask the operator about step 2. You should be able to formulate your own PEEMMM questions.

Question	What process element is being tested?
1. What kind of training did you receive?	People
2. Is there a procedure for taking samples? Where is it?	Methods
3. Do you identify the sample in any way? Do you have MFG-SP05 handy?	Methods

Continued

Continued

4.	What containers do you use for the sample? Who approves them?	Materials
5.	How do you know how much of a sample to take?	Measures
6.	How do you know when to take a sample? Do you keep a record?	Measures
7.	Is the sampling device approved? Calibrated?	Equipment
8.	How is the sampling device maintained? Does it ever break? What do you do then?	Equipment
9.	Does the area need to be clean when you take the sample? What about direct sunlight, how do you prevent it?	Environment
10.	Are there any safety issues when handling the molten sample? Have people been injured? What did they do?	Environment

In *process auditing*, you can follow the process flow and check interactions. The audit is now aligned with what the organization does to create value. Auditors can go from step to step as in this sampling process example and don't need to worry about stopping in manufacturing or limiting their questions to the lab. For internal audits, your only limit is not auditing your own area. You can conduct audits of simple or more complex processes, such as design processes, management scheduling, projects, new ventures, management review, production, human resource benefit distribution program, and so on. Process audits are a very important verification tool for high-risk processes, such as aircraft engine repair techniques, healthcare treatments, medical services, or nuclear device construction.

The PFD and process tree diagram are wonderful tools to aid the auditor, but there are other tools that can accomplish the same thing. In a pinch, an auditor can mark up a procedure to show process owners and check decision points. But PFDs are easier to follow and you won't find yourself wondering, "What did I mean by that note?" or "What is the scribbled name in the corner?"

Example conclusions:

- The process has (not) been effectively implemented.
- The process is (not) being maintained.
- Process owners are (not) familiar with the process steps and are (not) able to conduct the transaction with ease.
- The sequence of the process is (not) being followed.

Compare Performance to Objectives

Process inputs are converted to outputs to meet objectives. Every process has an objective or reason. Compare actual performance to the stated objective for the process. Objectives and goals are established to meet customer, business, environmental, and safety requirements. Objectives can come in many forms, such as output, variation, integrity, lack of contamination, size, and so on. The process could be falling short of some objectives and outperforming on others. If the process is falling short, ask what is being done to correct it. If they are exceeding objectives, should management *raise the bar* to improve competitiveness?

Auditors should test for the existence of objectives (goals) and the capability of the process to attain them. The effectiveness of a process is based on the extent to which plans are followed and plan results (objectives, goals) are achieved. Tracing tells us if plans are being followed and comparison of outputs against objectives tells us if results are achieved.

Example conclusions:

- The process is (not) achieving its objectives and is (not) effective.

- The process objectives are too broad and not contributing to the system.

- The process objectives are too narrow, resulting in extra cost and rework.

- No particular objectives have been set for this process resulting, in trial-and-error outputs.

This is valuable input to management for proper allocation of resources and determination of the effectiveness of the management/business system.

Risks

During process audits, auditors should continuously test the "what if" scenarios in their minds to identify probable failures. Every decision point in a process is an opportunity to apply error-proofing techniques. During a process audit, new sources of risk may be identified. Questions like the following may lead to the identification of new risks:

- What if they don't see the red switch?

- If this option is selected, could the product be misplaced?

- If delayed too long, could the material be a safety risk?

- If tarnished items are not failed, could they result in customer returns?

- Could the wrong instrument be used?

- Could patient IDs get transposed?

During process audits, auditors should be conducting continuous mistake proofing. Mistake proofing is about expecting the unexpected. Test scenarios in your mind and poke around to find weaknesses. If you think you found a weakness, test it on the process owner. If your finding is valid, what could be the negative consequences to the organization? A good auditor always has a mind-set to identify things that could go wrong (to prevent problems). However, auditors should remember that "what if" scenarios should be confined to sensible and relevant situations.

Example conclusions:

- There are unacceptable risks and work should be stopped.
- There are unavoidable risks, but there should be a contingency plan to minimize consequences.
- There are risks that can be avoided.
- Risks appear to be acceptable.

Neither people nor organizations can exist without risk. The kind and degree of risk must be managed. There may be safety (worker or customer injury), environmental (pollution, fines), financial (loss of revenue, excessive cost), and customer goodwill (loss of future sales) risks. Management needs to be informed of risks to the organization as input to the decision-making process. In some cases management is indifferent, and in other cases the potential consequences are unacceptable.

Optimization

Chapter 1 mentioned that all processes can be optimized to achieve their objectives. Every process has variables (speed, pressure, temperature, position, schedule, availability, skills, backups, space) that can be manipulated to optimize the process. *Optimization* is the most efficient use of resources to achieve objectives. You may be familiar with the optimization of manufacturing processes or techniques such as time studies. Optimization theory is a science within itself.

Optimization of processes may not be important in a compliance audit. The audit objectives for a compliance audit may be limited to ensuring that the documented process (procedure, work instruction, or other means) meets the audit criteria and that the documented process has been effectively implemented (people are following the rules). Compliance auditors could also be interested in objectives such as "no unsafe products will be shipped," "no recordables," "100 percent compliance." In other situations, optimization may not be important because the process is operating suboptimally by choice. Perhaps management is not concerned about optimization due to market conditions or the ROI. To optimize the process may be a low priority compared to other projects. However, optimization and bottleneck information may be important to management if you hear the auditee make statements similar to:

- We can't make them fast enough.
- We may need to go to a second shift or subcontract some work.
- Scheduling is very tight.
- There is a big backlog.
- Our working capital costs are through the roof.
- We are backed up, but there is nothing we can do.

Perhaps you are most familiar with optimizing manufacturing processes, but the same is true for service processes such as taking orders, entering transactions, issuing policies, and conducting treatments. Scenarios such as the retail store clerk example below are being addressed by service organizations.

Example: Retail store clerks

The number one job of the retail clerk is to wait on the customer. If there are no customers to wait on, the

---

Continued

Continued

clerk waits. Sometimes the clerk gets tired of waiting for the next customer and decides to talk to a fellow worker. When a customer does show up, the clerk may continue talking to the fellow employee until he/she gets to a good stopping point while the customer waits. In other cases, management notes the idle time, and assigns stocking, pricing or other duties to the clerk. When a customer shows up, the clerk may be preoccupied with his/her assignment and the customer waits for his/her needs to be addressed. The customer service objectives were not being achieved.

At one store, clerks were given assignments to fill in the idle time, but they were trained to stop work instantly to accommodate customer needs. Completing the assignment process was designed to be suboptimal (constant interruptions) but the objective to provide outstanding customer service process had a higher priority and added value. This is a win-win because the business if gaining productivity and the customer is being delighted (normally the customer expects to wait).

Processes can be optimized for specified output, safety, quality, and environmental constraints.

A process has a sequence of steps. When one step or activity is constraining or limiting the others, it is called a *bottleneck*. If you need more of something, eliminate the bottleneck. Bottlenecks can be the size of the container, speed of a machine, waiting for approval, cure time, and so on.

Process auditing techniques are very powerful. Process techniques can be used during system audits (such as ANSI/ISO/ASQ Q9001) to make them more effective. In a system audit you may not be able to trace from one end of the process to another, but you can trace selected orders, parts, or services throughout the various functions. That was the reason for getting the numbers during the tour (chapter 2). With your list of numbers (order, project, part, lot, customer, treatment), you can trace back and link processes.

SECTION II: USING PDCA FOR CONTROL AND ACDP FOR IMPROVEMENT

When auditing processes, auditors should always test for control. The PDCA technique can be used to test for the existence of control regardless of the documentation. Some performance standards require an organization to manage things or to ensure certain outcomes, but there are no specific requirements. Other performance standards contain a prescriptive list of requirements that the process controls must match or achieve. The PDCA technique can be used during process and system audits.

Control Risk

Standards, contracts, procedures, and documents frequently use the word *control*. It is one of those familiar terms that everyone seems to understand except that each person's understanding may be a little different. Yet, understanding control is central to the successful management of organizational risk. Standards help reduce risk if they are properly implemented and maintained. In fact, a standard may be thought of as a collection of controls that management implements for safety, quality, environment, and accounting systems to reduce risk.

Managers want to know that there is control over the important systems and processes of their organization. Auditors want to be able to verify that sufficient controls exist and report any shortcomings.

Control Criteria

Some have equated having a procedure with control: no procedure = no control. However, it is not that simple. Having a procedure does not necessarily mean there is control over a process.

In one audit, a truck driver for a transportation company was asked about the inspection process for his very expensive cargo. He responded, "Do you want to know what is in the procedure or what we actually do?" So, establishing a method is certainly an important process control tool, but does not guarantee there is control of the process. Management may use many different tools to ensure process objectives are realized.

Example: Management tools to enhance
control of a process

Control tools can include: procedures, checklists, PFDs,
schedules, reviews, policies, budgets, instructions,
forecasts, proforma statements, reports, flowcharts,
statistical techniques, records, software, devices,
internal auditing, training, and so on.

A simple, yet powerful, method for testing the
existence of controls regardless of the documentation is to use Walter Shewhart's plan-do-check-act
(PDCA) cycle. The PDCA cycle can be used as a
process technique to test for control (see Table 4.1).

Table 4.1 The PDCA (plan-do-check-act) process
technique.

---

1. **Plan:** A plan, procedure, or method is developed
   (establish what needs to be done).

2. **Do:** The plan, procedure, or method is followed
   (do what was planned).

3. **Check:** The plan, procedure, or method is
   monitored and measured against established
   criteria (know when it is done right).

4. **Act:** Action is taken to resolve the differences
   between expected and planned results (for
   example, analyze and adjust the process).

Test Controls

For management to control a process or activity, it must establish a predetermined method for that process. Without it, there is no basis to adjust or improve the process.

The predetermined method can be in any form and should reflect the level of process risk. Ways that a predetermined method can manifest itself include procedures, flowcharts, outlines, series of pictures, and training (consistent and verifiable). In most cases the predetermined method will be documented in some fashion (procedure, flowchart, and so on), but consistent verifiable practices provided through training may also be okay. Auditors can interview employees to check consistency and compare to training plans (lesson plans).

In one manufacturing situation, operators used their knowledge and skills to operate the process. When there were control problems, operators would judge the situation and make a number of changes to keep everything running smoothly. Every operator applied their years of experience to keep things on track. However, when it came time to improve the operation, no one could agree on the solution. They realized that each operator's skill and knowledge was different. They could not improve the operation because the operating method was a moving target (operators used different methods to address the same situation).

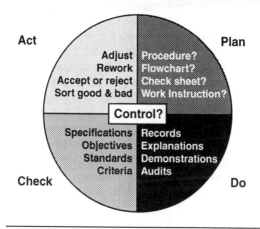

Figure 4.2 Plan-Do-Check-Act evidence.

So the first thing that had to be done was to establish a consistent method for operating. This is the *plan* part of the PDCA cycle. The predetermined plan can manifest itself as a procedure, agreed practice learned in training, a sample or example, or verbal and written instructions.

Now, just having a plan does not mean people will follow it. There must be some type of assurance (such as auditing, monitoring, retrievable records, or other means) that people follow the plan. This is the *do* part of the test cycle. Audit evidence may be found in a record or in the results of an interview with the auditee.

Just following a plan is not enough to establish management control because every process that needs to be controlled has at least two outcomes (good and bad, acceptable and unacceptable). Therefore, management must next determine the criteria or objectives for success or acceptance. The process must be measured and monitored against these criteria. As long as the process outputs match the predetermined acceptance criteria, the process does not need adjustment. This is the *check* part of the test cycle. Audit evidence of predetermined criteria could be specifications, records of checks, standards or objectives.

When the results do not match the acceptance criteria (output targets, goals), action must be taken. This is the *act* part of the test cycle. The action may be sorting good and bad product or making adjustments to the process to bring it back in line. Audit evidence of action could be rework, process adjustments, sorting bad stuff, rejections, and so on.

Testing for control of the process by using the PDCA technique can reveal fundamental flaws. The technique can be used to sort through complex situations to determine the existence and adequacy of the controls. *Process control* exists when the process or activity is planned, implemented, measured, and acted upon.

Interviewing for Control of the Process

You will not need a checklist to verify that a process is being controlled. A few simple interview questions will give you a wealth of information.

Such questions (see page 70) will not only answer many of your checklist questions, they will verify that process controls exist and are being maintained. The PDCA process technique is a very powerful method to test all processes. You can use this technique in every interview (see Figure 4.3) where someone is assigned a job or task.

However, we cannot stop here. Many new standards are requiring more than effective control. An organization's management or their customers are requiring improvement too. How can you test for improvement? If the organization's defects or errors were down last month, is that the audit evidence needed to verify there was improvement?

Test Improvement

A system or process must be changed to improve it. Improvement is not a matter of working harder or being more careful. If there is no change in some aspect of a system or process, the outcomes will always be the same. Avoid the fancy trend charts that show increases and, instead, look for change as the fundamental element that can verify improvement.

To test for improvement and preventive action, we can use PDCA again, only backwards, as the

Common process interview questions	Rationale
How do you know what to do?	Verifies existence of a predetermined method/plan. *Note: This may be noted on your PFD and can be crosschecked.*
How do you know the incoming stuff is okay to use?	Verifies how inputs are checked. *Note: This may be on your PFD or work instruction documents.*
Tell/Show me how you do it.	Verifies training and competency/knowledge. *Note: Records are also a good source of audit evidence to confirm people are doing what they said.*
How do you know that it is done right?	Verifies acceptance criteria have been established. *Note: This is vital for control and to ensure people take pride in their work.*
When it is not right, what do you do?	Verifies action is taken on the results. *Note: This closes the loop to ensure that the process meets objectives.*

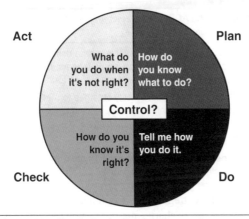

Figure 4.3 Plan it–Do it–Check it–Act on it.

ACDP (analyze-change-do-prosper) improvement cycle (see Table 4.4).

The purposes of a process audit and a system audit could be the same.

Many of us are familiar with what often happens to all the records and data collected—they are archived or put into storage, never to be seen again. For improvement to take place, the data must be analyzed for trends and weaknesses should be identified. This is the *analyze* step of the ACDP improvement cycle. By comparing results to goals and objectives, we analyze process data to identify risks, inefficiencies, opportunities for improvement,

Table 4.2 The ACDP (analyze-change-do-prosper) process technique.

1. **Analyze:** Analyze and evaluate data using chart techniques, comparisons, spreadsheets, tabulations, pictures, statistical techniques and so forth.

2. **Change**: Identify and justify changes to methods, application techniques, acceptance criteria, equipment, materials, technology and personnel.

3. **Do:** Implement change.

4. **Prosper:** Monitor improvement to show benefits in effectiveness (cost, opportunity and risk).

and negative trends. For example, audit evidence may be Pareto charts, matrices showing comparisons, histograms, or a failure mode effects analysis (FMEA). FMEA is a technique to look for potential problems so that preventive action can take place. By using the FMEA technique, organizations stay vigilant.

Changes could be in procedures or other elements of the process, such as the acceptance criteria or method of monitoring. Changes in equipment or technology may also be necessary for continual improvement. The merits of any change should be evaluated. This is the *change* part of the improvement test cycle. For example, evidence of a change of the system or process may be a capital request, project plan, or changes proposed as part of the FMEA analysis (see Figure 4.4).

The *do* step of the cycle is the implementation of the change. Auditors can verify that changes actually took place by reviewing documents and interviewing area personnel. For example, evidence of implementation may be audit reports or other records, as well as first hand observation.

Ongoing improvement should enable the organization to prosper in some manner. Improvement may be quantified as increased profitability, lower costs, lower exposure of the organization to risks, gain in market share or some other measure of improved effectiveness and efficiency. Sometimes organizations group changes and assess the effectiveness of

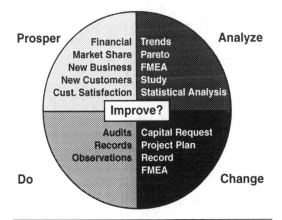

Figure 4.4 ACDP evidence.

several changes to the process. This assessment represents the *prosper* (or profit) step of the improvement test cycle. For example, evidence of improvement may be increased market share, new customer accounts, lower expenses, and so on (see Figure 4.4).

Auditing for Control and Improvement

When standards require control and improvement, both management and auditors need to know the components that must exist. It is management's job to establish and implement controls and ensure there is continual improvement. It is the auditor's job to gather audit evidence to verify conformance to requirements. In the absence of specific guidance (such as prescriptive requirements) in performance standards (required procedures, records or schedules), it is essential that management be able to demonstrate conformance to requirements.

Thus, the PDCA and ACDP cycles are process tools that can be used as guides to test for control and corrective or preventive actions. The PDCA cycle establishes control of a process. Control is required by standards and is a good business practice. The ACDP part of the cycle should be used to test for improvement. Some standards, such as ANSI/ISO/ASQ Q9001-2000 and ISO/TS 16949, require continual improvement. Improvement can only come from change.

In the next section, we discuss how to treat vague open-ended requirements.

SECTION III: AUDITING OPEN-ENDED REQUIREMENTS

Auditors need to be able to recognize and deal with requirements that are vague and subject to wide interpretation (open ended). For the auditor, it is important for all requirements to be verifiable and traceable regardless of their prescriptive nature. Open-ended requirements are found in standards such as ANSI/ISO/ASQ Q9001-2000 and its subsequent models (ISO/TS 16949, AS9100, TL9000) procedures, and work instructions.

Types of Open-ended Requirements Encountered

The use of open-ended requirements in some standards, procedures, work instructions is needed to ensure that the requirements are appropriate for different types of organizations. When requirements are too prescriptive, they can become too product or situation specific. For document users, the use of *open-ended requirements provides more flexibility* and can result in a more effective process. However, the more flexible requirements are subject to broader interpretation. There are four main types of open-ended requirements that auditors may encounter (see Table 4.3).

Table 4.3 Types of Open-ended Requirements.

Type I: Open-ended phrases/words	Type II: Generalized statements
Use of open-ended words subject to wide interpretation. Words such as *periodic*, *timely*, *readily*, *promptly*, *without undue delay*, and *based on importance* are not definitive. *Periodic* indicates repeatability but no frequency. *Timely* is relative to other undefined factors occurring concurrently or in the recent past or future. *Importance* is relative to the units being compared against.	Phrasing a requirement at a *generalized or abstract level* (for example, to manage or control a function or process). For example: The organization shall ensure *control* over such processes. The organization shall carry out production under *controlled* conditions. The organization shall *manage* the work environment.
Type III: Unclear or undefined words	**Type IV:** No tangibles specified use
Use of words that are not defined or are subject to multiple definitions, which can leave the auditor with *no basis for issuing a nonconformance.* For example: Top management must ensure the QMS is *suitable*. The organization shall make personnel aware of the *relevance* of their activities. *Exercise care* with customer property	A requirement lacking specified verifiable actions or outputs (for example, there is no requirement to define, document, record, schedule, review, and so on). *When there are no prescriptive requirements to audit against, audit findings could be perceived as subjective.* For example: The organization *shall preserve conformity* of the product. There is no requirement for a procedure or record or for management to control the process.

Requirements may be interpreted by the organization implementing the requirement, the audit organization, the auditor conducting the audit, or an independent board or committee convening for the purpose of making interpretations.

Type I: Open-ended phrases/words

Use of open-ended words subject to wide interpretation. Words such as *periodic, timely, readily, promptly*, without *undue delay*, and *based on importance* are not definitive.

Periodic indicates repeatability but no frequency. *Timely* is relative to other undefined factors occurring concurrently or in the recent past or future. *Importance* is relative to the units being compared against.

Type I: Open-ended Phrases/Words
Many Type I requirements are clarified by third-party audit organizations, such as registrars or government agencies that have oversight responsibility. For example, periodic management reviews may occur annually, or timely corrective action may be within 30 days. The planning of audits based on the importance of the process may be taken to mean auditing all elements annually. When interpretations are agreed upon (contract between audit organization and auditee organization), auditors are bound to audit against the interpretations. Official interpretations by auditing organizations or independent groups of specified requirements must also be adhered to.

It is not unusual to come across *as appropriate* or *as needed* during process audits. In the absence of other guidance, an auditor can ask the auditee for their interpretation and audit the organization against it. For example: What is *timely*? What is *without undue delay*? What is an *acceptable planned interval*? As long as you believe the organization is meeting the *intent* of the requirement and you corroborate it, it is okay (for example, as long as *as appropriate* means the same thing to everyone making those decisions).

Interpretations can also vary from industry to industry. A requirement to be prompt in the medical device or nuclear industry may be applied differently for a soap manufacturer or boat company.

Type II: Generalized statements

Phrasing a requirement at a *generalized or abstract level* (for example, to manage or control a function or process).

For example: The organization shall ensure *control* over such processes. The organization shall carry out production under *controlled* conditions. The organization shall *manage* the work environment.

Type II: Generalized Statements to Control or Manage

There are overall general requirements to manage or control processes. These function-level requirements can be very powerful. However, if organizations don't know how to implement the requirement and auditors don't know how to audit against it, the requirement may be ignored as fluff or un-auditable.

Normally, it is only when an auditor must prove the negative (issue a nonconformity) that guidance issues surface. When is there lack of control? When is a process not being adequately managed? What evidence will withstand the scrutiny of the exit meeting and a subsequent review, if a nonconformity is appealed or questioned? Auditors want to be right the first time and not withdraw a nonconformity or noncompliance once they have determined one is justified. It is in everyone's best interest that the basis for a nonconformity be clear and not appear to be a subjective opinion.

Auditors have at least two approaches that they can use to audit generalized requirements to control a process or activity. They can use: (1) PDCA process techniques (discussed previously in this chapter) or (2) requirement techniques referencing a standard such as ANSI/ISO/ASQ Q9001-2000, ANSI/ISO 14001, or ISO/TS 16949. Clause 7.5.1 of ANSI/ISO/ASQ Q9001-2000 has a handy list of specific things to consider for controlling an operation/process. Auditors can make up a checklist (see Appendix B: Process Control Checklist) of the specific requirements from clause 7.5.1 and determine which control conditions exist and do not exist.

Type III: Unclear or undefined words

Use of words that are not defined or are subject to multiple definitions, which can leave the auditor with *no basis for issuing a nonconformance.*

For example: Top management must ensure the QMS is *suitable.* The organization shall make personnel aware of the *relevance* of their activities. *Exercise care* with customer property.

Type III: Unclear or Undefined

Use of unclear or undefined terms is becoming less and less of an issue. Many standard users are more familiar with terminology and standard writers are publishing definitions to make the standards more user friendly. However, if word definitions are a problem, auditors can seek guidance from audit organization management.

Auditors can also help themselves by researching other standards (such as ANSI/ISO/ASQ Q9000-2000 or ISO 14050 vocabulary standards) and guidelines or from studying audit organization documents. Also, the application of some words may be defined by industry-specific documents. And don't forget a dictionary. A good, up-to-date dictionary can be very helpful.

Type IV: No tangibles specified

A requirement lacking specified verifiable actions or outputs (that is, there is no requirement to define, document, record, schedule, review, and so on). *When there are no prescriptive requirements to audit against, audit findings could be perceived as subjective.*

For example: The organization *shall preserve conformity* of the product.

There is no requirement for a procedure or record or for management to control the process.

Type IV: No Tangibles Specified

Type IV open-ended requirements do not require the organization to manage or control and have no specific auditable requirements. Verification of conformance to type IV requirements is challenging for auditors and audit organizations. This is particularly true for traditional compliance assessments where supplemental guidance may be appropriate. When type IV requirements appear, auditors must challenge the auditee to explain how they comply.

For example, clause 7.5.5 of ANSI/ISO/ASQ Q9001-2000 states that the organization shall preserve the conformity of the product. There is no requirement to plan, establish, determine, specify, document, maintain, manage, schedule, control, review, assess, or record. The requirement is more like a goal, and the organization has to come up with an approach to achieve the goal (requirement).

To audit the type IV open-ended clauses, the auditor can verify that the organization conforms to the intent of the requirements of the standard by using PDCA process techniques. The auditor must seek to determine the existence of a process, how it was planned and implemented, and its outcomes (remember the PDCA approach discussed earlier).

Too Many Open-ended Requirements

If during your audit preparation and completing the PFD you observe significant issues regarding open-ended requirements, you can request that the auditee provide their interpretations before you start the audit. For example, you may have come across a perfectly written procedure or work instruction that says nothing and makes no commitments to anything. Perfect in that it may meet a requirement for a procedure but requires nothing of the auditee or process owner. Such situations do not add value or meet the intent of a requirement to control a process (see sections earlier in this chapter regarding techniques to evaluate controls).

Summary

To audit open-ended requirements, auditors will need to be ready to use a diverse set of audit techniques to verify conformance and to provide traceability. This section provides auditors with additional strategies and techniques for addressing open-ended type requirements found in conformity standards and organization documents. *If a standard does not prescribe an approach, the organization must establish an approach* and be audited against it.

Next is a brief chapter on auditing to ANSI/ISO/ ASQ Q9001-2000. The reorganization, process approach, and new requirements of ANSI/ISO/ASQ Q9001 need addressing because they have caused confusion in the auditing world.

Chapter 5

Auditing to ANSI/ISO/ASQ Q9001-2000

The style and approach of ANSI/ISO/ASQ Q9001-2000 necessitates the need for auditors to use process auditing methods. The use of tracing, flowcharting, and PDCA evaluation techniques align with management systems that have been deployed using the process approach. The *use of process auditing techniques* in both system and process audits is needed to *support the process approach design* (sequencing, linking, and measuring) and to *collect audit evidence* to verify conformity to requirements.

Important note for all students

Though many of you may not have an ANSI/ISO/ASQ Q9001-2000 QMS, you may encounter similar strategies in derivative or future standards. Knowing the strategies and how to deal with them will make you a more skillful auditor. This chapter has been included because auditors need to be aware of standard style changes.

Need for New Auditing Techniques

The most significant things about ANSI/ISO/ASQ Q9001-2000 compared to prior versions are the strategic and tactical changes (see Figure 5.1). The ANSI/ISO/ASQ Q9001-2000 version has very few new requirements compared to the prior version, but the remodeling of the standard has organizations revisiting their deployment strategy and assessing the need for QMS culture change.

The strategic changes include: the process approach in the design of the standard, customization of the QMS based on user application, reduction of required documentation, and use of open-ended requirements.

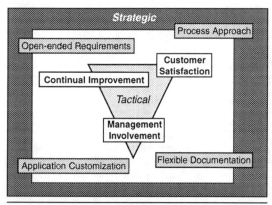

Figure 5.1 Strategic and tactical changes.

The tactical changes include: continual improvement as an auditable requirement, an aim to achieve customer satisfaction, and verification of management's increased leadership and involvement.

SECTION I: STRATEGIC CHANGES

Process Approach

A process transforms inputs into outputs. Thinking in terms of a series of activities that lead to a desired result (objective) is a more effective and efficient way of managing. This is the process approach. It is how we normally do things or should do things compared to the "ready–fire–aim" method. Functions such as manufacturing or operations may be organized using the process approach. There will be processes within processes to support the function. ANSI/ISO/ASQ Q9001-2000, clause 4.1, is the key to implementing the process approach for the management system. You can make up a handy requirements list from the ANSI/ISO/ASQ 9001-2000, clause 4.1 a) through f) requirements (see Appendix C).

Clauses 4.1 a, 4.1 b, and 4.1 c are the key to successful implementation of the process approach. The clauses require: a) identification of processes needed for the management system, b) determination of the sequence and

Continued

Continued

interaction of the processes, and
c) determination of the criteria and
methods to control the processes
effectively. When auditing, auditors
should verify organizations have
established and defined the processes
necessary to provide their product(s)
and/or service(s) to customers.

QMS Application

ANSI/ISO/ASQ Q9001 has a built in flexibility to
tailor the standard to the nature of the user organization. This subjectivity will require auditors to
judge whether the decisions made by the user of
the standard are applicable or not. Auditors must
also determine if ongoing changes in the business
or business environment necessitate the addition or
deletion of applicable clauses to the QMS.

Fewer Required Documents

Many standards (not only ANSI/ISO/ASQ Q9001)
are criticized for requiring documents that do not
add value. Comments about ANSI/ISO/ASQ
Q9001-1994 being a *paper mill* or being responsible for the destruction of the Brazilian rain forest
are common.

The ANSI/ISO/ASQ Q9001-2000 strategy of
requiring fewer documents addresses one of the
main complaints about an ANSI/ISO/ASQ Q9001

QMS. However, the lack of required procedures (only six are required) burdens the auditor to determine if the methods used by the organization meet ANSI/ISO/ASQ Q9001 requirements. For there to be control, there must be a predetermined method. An auditor must seek out the predetermined method and assess its adequacy to the ANSI/ISO/ASQ 9001 requirements (chapter 4).

Use of Open-ended Requirements

The standard also includes many open-end requirements (nonprescriptive) to accommodate different industry sectors (both product and service) as well as different sized organizations. The structure of the ANSI/ISO/ASQ 9001 standard is adaptable to all organizations and can be an effective tool for achieving quality objectives and customer satisfaction. However, the open-ended nature of some requirements are subject to wider interpretation and make it harder to collect indisputable audit evidence to justify a nonconformity.

SECTION II: TACTICAL CHANGES

Achieve Customer Satisfaction

The achievement of customer satisfaction is an integral part of the ANSI/ISO/ASQ Q9001 standard. This strategy represents an expansion beyond the previous focus of adherence to procedures. Who cares if you followed all your procedures if your customers are unhappy or your product is unsafe?

According to the ANSI/ISO/ASQ Q9000 vocabulary standard, the definition of *customer* includes internal and external customers of the product or service. Organizations may provide products or services to other divisions or departments within the same organization as internal customers. Simply, the organization or person receiving the product or service is the customer.

The two main clauses auditors must assess related to customer satisfaction are clause 5.2 (Customer focus) and 8.2.1 (Customer satisfaction). Clause 5.2 is under management responsibility but is linked to other clauses in the standard.

It is clear that clause 7.2.1 addresses determination of customer requirements and that clause 8.2.1 addresses *customer satisfaction*. If there is a nonconformity related to clause 7.2.1 or 8.2.1, there could be a nonconformity linked to 5.2, too.

ANSI/ISO/ASQ Q9001-2000, 5.2 Customer focus

Top management shall ensure that customer *requirements are determined* and are met with the aim of *enhancing customer satisfaction* (see 7.2.1 and 8.2.1).

Example interview questions for top management using process techniques:

Questions for clause 5.2	Possible answer
Do you have a method or plan for ensuring customer requirements are determined and met?	Besides our order entry guidelines, we conduct FMEA on products and services to uncover potential requirements, and discuss it at every sales and departmental meeting.
How do you know your plan or method is being followed?	I review the audit results for the order entry department, approve the sales meeting agenda, and the performance manager monitors the FMEA program.
What are the acceptance criteria or objective(s)?	Our objective is to meet 100% of the customer requirements and 100% customer satisfaction.
If you are not meeting your objective, what do you do?	I get a weekly exception report. If we cannot meet requirements, we don't ship. Either we replace the product from another warehouse or advise the customer for action. Additionally, analyzed information is used as input to our preventive action process.

The key to meeting the ANSI/ISO/ASQ Q9001 clause 5.2 requirements is the involvement and awareness of top management.

Besides clause 5.2, auditors must also be able to verify clause 8.2.1 on measuring customer satisfaction. This clause has some prescriptive *shall* requirements that auditors can verify. Check the example questions below.

How to get the customer's perception is not well understood. Customer perception information is subjective and customer criticism can be very painful at

Example interview questions taken from specified requirements:

Questions for clause 8.2.1	Possible evidence
1. Is customer satisfaction one of the measures of QMS performance?	It is reported and reviewed at management meetings.
2. Does the organization monitor the customer's perception that their requirements are being met?	Customer feedback information comes from the customer directly and survey questions are linked to customer requirements (versus marketing-type surveys).
3. Have methods been defined for obtaining and using the customer satisfaction information?	There is an information collection plan (outline) of what information is being monitored, steps for collecting it, and how it will be analyzed and reported.
4. *Auditor Information Note: Management review should include plans for acting on the customer feedback information.*	Check management review minutes/reports.

times. No one strategy, such as *top box* (see Glossary), is appropriate for all products, services, and organization sectors. Organizations that learn how to measure customer satisfaction in an effective manner and respond to customers are going to prosper.

The same concept of knowing and matching customer requirements could be applied internally since every process output has a customer. Going beyond minimum compliance, organizations could apply the customer satisfaction controls to all internal customers (department to department, section to section) and to all interested parties, such as stockholders, bankers, and community leaders.

Continual Improvement

Another major complaint about the ANSI/ISO/ASQ Q9001-1994 conformance standard was that it did not require improvement. As long as an organization had a good nonconforming product control process to ensure bad product did not make it to the customer, they could pass an ANSI/ISO/ASQ Q9001 audit with flying colors.

Author's comment about compliance and continual improvement

The introduction of the requirement to continually improve sent a shockwave through the regulatory

---

Continued

Continued

bodies. They would say, "This was too much of a change and, besides, it is not enforceable and we cannot shut down companies just because they don't continually improve." The critiques are correct, but not every requirement violation contained in FAA, FDA, and EPA regulations would result in shutting down an organization. Perhaps regulated organizations *should* be required to improve. Perhaps it is in the public's best interest if they receive the safest, most affordable, and most reliable products and services available.

The key to verification of continual improvement is identification of organization change, such as using the ACDP technique in chapter 6. Specifically, organizations are to continually improve the effectiveness of the QMS (ANSI/ISO/ASQ Q9001-2000, clause 8.5.1). In order to comply with this requirement you need to know what effectiveness means and what is included in the quality management system, as opposed to the safety system or business management system. Definitions of effectiveness and other terms have been provided in the glossary in the back of the book. In practical terms, a QMS would be effective if process steps are followed and output objectives are accomplished.

As an auditor, you could accept any change that improves the quality of the product, service, or system as audit evidence of continual improvement.

Continual improvement could be changes that result in narrowing product or service variation, better meeting customer or regulatory requirements, and changes to the QMS that may lower product or service risk. Since ANSI/ISO/ASQ Q9001-2000 is a conformance standard and excludes requirements to improve efficiency, auditors should not accept improvements made solely for reducing cost or improving efficiency. Only the ANSI/ISO/ASQ Q9004 guideline standard for improving business performance requires organizations to be more efficient.

A place to look for evidence would be the output of management review. You can also evaluate corrective and preventive actions.

Management Involvement

There are several requirements for top management commitment to the QMS and involvement that must be verified by an auditor. The ANSI/ISO/ASQ Q9001-2000 is designed to increase management involvement. In fact, there are several prescriptive requirements that auditors can use to assess management's involvement, such as those found in ANSI/ISO/ASQ Q9001-2000, clause 5.1. When you use a checklist, evaluating management commitment is straightforward.

Example of a clause 5.1 requirements list:

Clause 5.1 requirements list for demonstrating top management commitment

Is there evidence of top management commitment by:

a) Communicating the importance of meeting customer and regulatory requirements

b) Establishing a quality policy

c) Ensuring there are quality objectives

d) Conducting management reviews

e) Ensuring availability of resources

[Verify a) through e). Look at the quality policy; verify management reviews are taking place and top management is involved. Verify that a) is linked to 5.5.2 c).]

The organizations that did only the minimum to get an ANSI/ISO/ASQ Q9001 certificate may balk at the additional management commitment requirements. Management may even re-evaluate their need to keep their registration. For other organizations, the extra management involvement may be just what was needed for management to take ISO 9001 registration seriously and see how it can add value.

Summary

The standard is requiring the user to think in terms of the quality management system being a set of processes and processes within processes. Auditors must align their auditing techniques to the process approach for maximum user benefit.

There is no specific requirement in ANSI/ISO/ASQ Q9001 or ANSI/ISO/ASQ QE19011 to conduct process audits or use process audit techniques. For internal auditing, the ANSI/ISO/ASQ Q9001 standard only requires that the auditor audit the QMS against ANSI/ISO/ASQ Q9001 requirements and the QMS requirements established by the organization. Auditors should consider conducting process audits and using process techniques because it is an effective audit method and better supports the *process approach* of the standard.

Now it is time to bring your audit evidence together and to report your findings to management.

Chapter 6

Analyze and Report Findings

You should be finished with steps 1 through 5, and now you are ready to report your results. We will assume you already know the basics of analyzing and categorizing data from an audit; in this chapter we will discuss what could be different.

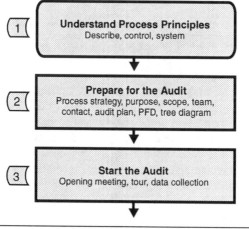

Process auditing steps 1–6.

Continued

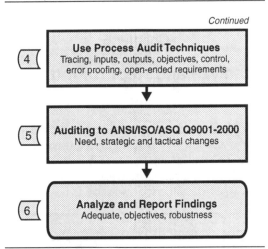

Continued

Process auditing steps 1–6.

Analyze Data

Now review your audit evidence to sort and identify relevant data and its importance (see Figure 6.1). Is the data relevant to the purpose and scope? Does it represent a minor defect or a potential systemic problem? Is it a nonconformity or improvement point?

If you are like most auditors, you will have a set of notes taken during the audit. Your notes may be recorded in several places such as on your checklist, listed on your log sheets, or written on your PFD or tree diagram. While you are auditing, you need to

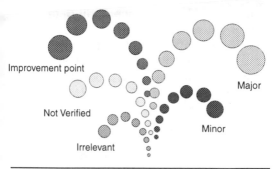

Improvement point

Major

Not Verified

Minor

Irrelevant

Figure 6.1 Sort your data.

record the information as soon as possible. Many auditors record the data by the first means available. If you are using your PFD to ask interview questions, you may end up recording responses on the PFD rather than taking the time to find the right checklist question comment box. You may also have collected audit evidence such as blank forms, copies of records, or reports or documents.

TIP

Go through your notes and mark important observations. You may use some type of code or key such as a circled star means a potential minor nonconformance/finding, two circled stars means a major nonconformance/finding. You can use the document paragraph numbers to link observations that relate to the same effect or finding.

Compliance/Conformance Audit Data

In chapter 4, you may recall, we evaluated the process for adherence to prescribed methods, assessing the adequacy of controls, identification of risks, and process optimization. The approach for analyzing the data may vary depending on whether the purpose of the audit was only to verify compliance or to assess performance improvement as well.

First, the audit data should verify step-by-step adherence to requirements. Are the rules being followed (see Figure 6.2, Follow the rules)? If the observed process is not the same as that required

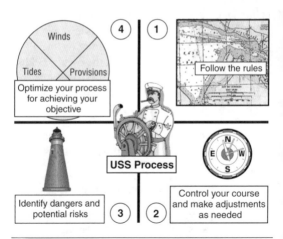

Figure 6.2 Tests.

by the standard, work instruction, or regulation, then the noncompliance should be reported. For a compliance audit, management wants to know if the rules are being followed.

Next, your data should indicate whether process outputs are being achieved. Is the process on-course (see Figure 6.2, Control your course)? For the compliance audit, you will be interested in objectives that relate to compliance issues, such as safe product, contaminant-free, purity, 100 percent compliance, no test failures, and so on. You, as the auditor, cannot collect the data yourself, but you can ensure that the auditee is assessing their process against the appropriate objectives/goals.

Your investigation could also reveal process control gaps. *Control gaps* may represent risk to the organization for potential regulatory issues. *Control requirements* may stem from documents such as work instructions or regulations. You may also need agreement on the interpretation of the word *control* in order to issue a noncompliance for inadequate control.

Risks may be reported for potential quality, safety, or environmental failures. What are the risks (see Figure 6.2, Identify dangers)? Product safety is about customer safety as well as employee safety. As the auditor, you are not able to assess the accept-ability of the risk to the organization. It is up to management to determine follow-up actions to address risk issues. You can report any additional observations that will help management, such as the frequency of the occurrence (it happened once or it happened three times during the audit) or assessments made by the process owner (this is critical, it always gets fixed later in the process, it has a negligible effect, and so on).

Normally, compliance-focused audits are not concerned with optimization of the process (see Figure 6.2, Optimize your process). The process rules are not subject to change and a lot of energy goes into ensuring that the rules are always followed.

Performance Audit Data

Besides the step-by-step adherence to requirements, auditors should assess the effectiveness of the process steps. Process performance observations may include redundancies, inefficiencies, waste, unnecessary rework, and non-value-added steps or tests.

Experts state that if a process is meeting output objectives, it is an effective process. Management determines the objectives and goals. Your data should indicate whether the process owners are measuring results against the stated objectives/goals. They should know if the *process objectives are being achieved.*

Example Output Objectives

Purity	Identified	Satisfied
Dimension	Marked	Meets requirements
Level	Volume	On-time

Assessment of effectiveness should include determination that the controls are adequate and that the process is capable. In our modern world, the means no longer justify the end. For example, adding three inspectors at the end of the line to ensure only good product goes to the customer may meet output objectives but increases costs. A truly effective process is balanced between the output goals and the capability of the process. Some organizations include both output objectives and process performance objectives.

Example Process Performance Objectives

Right the first time	Less scrap	Reduced sorting time
No rework	No expediting	Eliminate re-grading
Fewer repeat tests	Narrow variation	

As a process auditor, you have some knowledge of the process but still must rely on the process owner to measure the effectiveness of the process. If you observe an ineffective process or the process owner is not measuring effectiveness, you should put it in your report.

Identification of potential risks to the process or organization is an important input for performance improvement. Continuous mistake proofing during the audit may bear ample fruit for any preventative action program. You should report all risks that you believe could be significant. If you don't believe you are qualified to assess the significance (potential negative consequences) of the risk, you can report all your observations or verbally share what you consider to be nominal or negligible. Your quantification of the risk would be helpful to management.

All processes can be optimized. Every process is controlled by a set of variables. The variables (inputs) can be balanced to maximize the process objectives. Information about optimization of the process, or set of processes, is important when the process is operating at near apparent capacity. Identification of process bottlenecks could result in increases of capacity to better meet requirements. Identification of process steps with excess capacity could result in arrangements that better meet requirements. For example, if step 1 of a 3-step process has significant excess capacity, steps 2 and 3 could be outsourced or given to toll operators. Information about potential process inefficiencies, surplus capacity, or bottlenecks would be helpful to management.

Sometimes there is no bottleneck because all the process steps are evenly balanced and changing one or two steps will not effect the output or quality of the process overall. In other cases, where market or other constraints require processes to operate at a suboptimal level (limited warehouse space, spotty demand, working capital limits, or controls), there is no apparent bottleneck. There is no need for an auditor to conjure up what-if scenarios to point out potential process bottlenecks if it is not relevant to the situation.

System Audits

When conducting management system audits, auditors should use process auditing techniques. If you are able to trace a product, project, or service through the process, you can make observations about adherence to QMS and process steps, adequacy of controls, potential risks, and opportunities for optimization (Compliance Audit Data and Performance Audit Data).

The Report

The report must be consistent with the purpose and scope. An internal process audit of a work instruction can be one or two pages. An external audit of several processes could be 10 or more pages. The report size may depend on whether it was a process audit of the 250-ton stamping machine, or all the stamping machines, or the assembly line or manufacturing process. Larger reports are more formal and their requirements are covered in most standard audit training programs, and in books such as *The Quality Audit Handbook* (ASQ Quality Press).

In our example report form (also see Appendix D), the audit report is a single page (see Figure 6.3). It is a memo format (To-From-CC) with standard identifiers (number, dates, area audited). We have combined the audit report and corrective action record so that all the follow-up is in one place. There is space for overall findings and all the rows are expandable (use electronic forms so that rows can be expanded to fit the information). A process audit report can be very simple and functional. Individual problems and nonconformities can be listed along with the traceable requirement (paragraph, document, objective, and so on). If the report receivers need to have background information, attach the audit plan. If additional information is needed by the auditee, client, or audit program manager, it should have been agreed upon in the preparation phase of the audit.

The detailed results can be both isolated incidents and systemic issues. It is not uncommon for compliance process audit reports to be a list of

Process Audit Report and Corrective Action Record

		Audit Date(s):		Report Date:		
To:						
From:				Audit No:		
Copy:				Auditor(s):		
Process Audited:						
Purpose:						
Standard-Procedure-Instruction:						
Overall Findings / Conclusion:						
	Report Details			Status			
No.	Finding/ Nonconformance	Ref # Para.	Follow-up Action Remedial and/or Corrective Action	Planned Completion Date	Plan Approved	Actual Completion Date	Verified

Figure 6.3 Report form.

defects compared to a procedure or work instruction. This type of defect reporting can promote *remedial (containment)* actions instead of corrective action. For modern day auditing (value-added) we need to group observations under systemic findings when possible.

Record your findings in order of importance. Some findings represent high risk to the organization, while others represent low risk. You can classify your finds as either major–minor or you could set up a rating system. A rating could be something like A items require immediate action (high risk); B items need to be planned and addressed in the near future, such as 90 days (medium risk); and C items need to be planned for a future date, such as the next change over, the annual document review, the next six months, and so on (low risk).

Using software for reporting is a great tool, but some software is too inflexible. Avoid software that does not allow you the space to report complete information or forces you to report irrelevant or unnecessary information. Word processing software allows for structure and expandability. Required information can be listed in boxes and then the boxes can be sized to fit the appropriate amount of information.

The report should include a conclusion. It is important for auditors to share overall assessment of the situation. Overall conclusions may be:

- Procedures and instructions are not being followed as originally intended.

- The process appears to be operating effectively. No major problems were identified.

- There are significant business risks that must be addressed if this process is going to continue to operate.

- The process is compliant. However, planned changes represent considerable risk to the process such that I recommend another process audit be conducted in six months.

- The controls for the process are not adequate such that the safety of the product is assured.

- The process is effective overall, but there were several process changes that have not been implemented.

- The process is achieving the established objectives, but process bottlenecks have resulted in several inefficiencies.

In the compliance world of auditing, you can report on the effective implementation and maintenance of a process but not efficiency. In the performance world of auditing, you can report on overall effectiveness and efficiency of the process. In the *business world*, all the information is needed to better manage risk.

There should be enough information in the report such that any reasonable person would come to the conclusions that you did. You should back up finding statements with relevant data and give examples of what you observed.

Before you dot the last *i* or cross the final *t*, confirm two things: (1) that you were able to verify the audit criteria (requirements, policy, promises) and (2) that the audit sample was sufficient. If these are true, you will feel confident and it will show in your report. If not, you need to report any gaps or areas needing additional oversight.

The lead auditor should sign the report. Your organization will need to determine if additional approval or reviews of the report are required.

Closing Meeting

As required by good audit practices, there must be a closing meeting. The size, formality, and length will vary depending on the purpose, scope, and findings of the process audit. Most process audit closing meetings will be very short. The process owners and decision makers should be at the closing meeting because they control the resources needed to address your findings. Follow standard exit meeting protocols such as those found in *The Quality Audit Handbook*.

Whether you provide a draft or final report at the exit meeting depends on what is most effective for the situation. For an internal process audit in an open and trusting culture that uses audits as a management tool for improvement, auditors may give the auditee the final report at the closing meeting. Copies of the report should go to the client and other agreed-upon interested parties. This is both effective and efficient. For more formal third- and second-party audits, standard conventions should be followed. The auditor can provide a draft of the findings and later send the final report to the client for distribution.

Ending the Process Audit

The audit ends when the audit plan has been fully executed (completed) and the audit report is issued. Auditors may or may not be involved with any required follow-up activities. Audit findings should result in corrective or preventive actions. The corrective or preventive actions may be addressed by the client, special teams, or as-a-matter-of-course for the auditee. The proper management of the follow up actions is addressed in texts such as *After the Quality Audit* and *The Quality Audit Handbook*. The follow-up actions are core to benefiting from the audit process. I like to think of the audit as only being half over until all the findings are addressed.

Later, you may be asked to follow the audit and verify the promised corrective and preventive actions. Verification may be done as a follow-up audit or as part of the next audit of that process.

Closing Remarks

Process auditing and the use of process techniques during process and system audits are very powerful. It is better to audit processes according to their functionality (form, fit, and function) rather than by isolated elements.

Glossary

acceptance criteria: Predetermined desirable characteristics that will meet customer requirements.

attribute data: 1. A quality characteristic classified as either conforming or nonconforming to specifications.[5] 2. Data requiring a count of discrete measurements, such as good and bad,[6] used when variable measurements are not possible (color, missing parts, scratches, damage, smoothness) or where go/no-go gauges are preferred over taking actual measurements (hole diameter range, over/under, align with template).

audit: 1. Systematic, independent, and documented process for obtaining evidence and evaluating it objectively to determine the extent to which audit criteria are fulfilled.[7] 2. A planned, independent, and documented assessment to determine whether agreed-upon requirements are being met. Ref. ASQC Quality Auditing Technical Committee (now the Quality Audit Division of American Society for Quality). *See* quality audit.

audit evidence: Records, statements of fact, or other information that are relevant to the audit criteria and are verifiable.[8] Note: *verifiable* in the meaning that it can be cross-checked.

audit plan: Description of the on-site activities and arrangements for an audit.[9] Simply, it is a plan for the audit that can take on any form convenient for the auditors and auditee.

auditee: Organization being audited.[8,10]

auditor: 1. Person qualified to perform audits.[10] 2. Person with the competence to conduct an audit.[7]

best practice: Something observed that is outstanding and should be shared. Sometimes called *noteworthy achievement* or *positive practice*.

capacity: 1. The power or ability to hold, receive, or accommodate. 2. Capacity is the estimated maximum level of output that

meets objectives of a process on a sustained
or ongoing basis. 3. The facility or power to
produce, perform or deploy. (*Webster's Ninth
Collegiate Dictionary*, Springfield, MA:
Merriam-Webster, 1990).

client, audit: The organization or person
requesting the audit.[7]

competent: 1. Having requisite or adequate ability
or qualities. 2. Having the capacity to function
or respond in a particular way. Competence
denotes having acquired and using one's
formal education, training, skills, and
experience. 3. Demonstrated ability to apply
knowledge and skills.[7]

complex process audit: Auditing processes
within processes at the procedure or function
level. A complex transformation, such as
manufacturing (from raw material to finished
good), operating (service operations),
assembling (assembly line), and so on.

concern, audit: Issues that are potential
nonconformities.[7]

conduct: A mode or standard of personal behavior,
especially as based on moral principles.[11]

conformity: Fulfillment of a requirement.[7]

continual improvement: Continual improvement is thought (by some regulators) to be step-wise improvement, as opposed to continuous improvement that is thought to be perpetual or constant improvement. For that reason the word continual as opposed to continuous is used in the new ANSI/ISO/ASQ Q9000-2000 standard. Common dictionaries do not support the distinction made by the standard writers. Continual improvement is a recurring process of enhancing the environmental management system in order to achieve improvements in overall environmental performance consistent with the organization's environmental policy.[12]

continuous improvement: Includes action taken throughout an organization to increase the effectiveness and efficiency of activities and processes in order to provide added benefits to the customer and organization. It is considered a subset of total quality management and operates according to the premise that organizations can always make improvements. Continuous improvement can also be equated with reducing process variation.[13]

control: 1. Power or authority to manage, exercising directing or restraining influence (Webster's Ninth Collegiate Dictionary). 2. Regulate (ANSI/ISO/ASQ Q9000-2000 Product support package N526). 3. *Effective control* is when management directs events in such a manner as to provide assurance that the organization's objectives and goals will be achieved (statement from *Internal Auditing Standards* glossary). 4. Control is when the requirements of clause 7.5.1 of ANSI/ISO/ASQ Q9000-2000 have been implemented and maintained.

correction: Action taken to eliminate a detected nonconformity. Correction may involve repair, rework, or regrading.

corrective action: 1. Action taken to eliminate the causes of an *existing* nonconformity, defect, or other undesirable situation in order to prevent *recurrence* (reactive). 2. Action taken to eliminate the cause of a detected nonconformity or other undesirable situation.[7]

corroborate: 1. Confirm, verify, authenticate. 2. To support with evidence or authority, to make certain.[14]

customer: Organization or person that receives a product.[7]

customer goodwill: An intangible financial asset. Customer goodwill may manifest itself as repeat business, referrals, and brand loyalty. The excess of the purchase price of a business over estimated value of net assets exclusive of goodwill.

defect: Nonfulfillment of an intended usage requirement or *reasonable expectation*, including one concerned with safety.[10]

directed sampling: Directed (or judgmental) sample selection is based on the auditor's judgment or direction given to the auditor. The auditor may purposely bias the sample selection to only high-risk or problem areas.

discovery sampling: A random sampling technique that uses no methodology. Easy to use but could result in biased samples.

effectiveness: 1. Extent to which planned activities are realized and planned results achieved.[7] 2. The consideration or balance between achieving the desired results (the product) and how they were achieved (the process).[15] 3. The degree to which objectives are achieved in an efficient and economical manner.[16]

efficiency: 1. Relationship between the result achieved and resources used.[7]
2. Accomplishes objectives and goal with optimal use of resources.[17]

ethical: 1. Of or relating to ethics. 2. Involving or expressing moral approval or disapproval. 3. Conforming to accepted professional standards of conduct.[11]

ethics: 1. The discipline dealing with what is good and bad and with moral duty and obligation. 2. (a) a set of moral principles or values; (b) a theory or system of moral values; (c) the principles of conduct governing an individual or a group; (d) a guiding philosophy.[11]

environment: Surroundings in which an organization operates, including air, water, land, natural resources, flora, fauna, humans, and their interrelations.

evidence: Data (records, responses to questions, observations, and so on) that can be verified. Also called *objective evidence*. Evidence

can be qualitative and/or quantitative.
See audit evidence.

finding: 1. Deficiency found during an audit.
2. The result of an investigation. 3. A type
of audit result that makes a statement about
systemic problems. 4. Results of the
evaluation of the collected audit evidence
against audit criteria.[8]

flowchart: A picture of the separate steps of a
process in sequential order. Sometimes called
a process flow diagram or service map.[18]

gig list: A list of minor infractions.

haphazard sampling: Selecting a sample with
a goal to be as random as practical and be
representative of the population being
examined.

improvement point: Areas of ineffectiveness or
poor process efficiency.

inspection: Activities such as measuring,
examining, and testing of characteristics
against predetermined acceptance criteria
to determine conformity.

isolated incident: An occurrence of an action or situation felt as a separate unit of experience. Set apart from others. Not likely to reoccur. Not inherent in the process or system design.

method: 1. A plan or system of action, inquiry, analysis, and so on. 2. Order or system of one's actions. 3. The manner in which one acts, as in conducting business.[19] Note: methodologies may be a body of methods, rules, and postulates employed by a discipline, a particular procedure, or set of procedures [www.webster.com (defunct)].

noncompliance: Term used in place of a nonconformity; popular in the regulated industries.

nonconformity: Nonfulfillment of a specified requirement,[10] or nonfulfillment of a requirement.[8]

objective: 1. Uninfluenced by emotion, surmise, or personal prejudice. 2. Based on observable phenomena, presented factually.[20]

objective evidence: Data supporting the existence or verification of something.[7]

observation: Something viewed. During an audit or investigation, an observation could be information that may be evidence to support audit conclusions.

organization: Group of people and facilities with an arrangement of responsibilities, authorities, and relationships.[7] Note: where *supplier* was used in the 1994 version of the ISO standard, *organization* is now used.

PDCA: The plan–do–check–act (PDCA) cycle was first developed by Shewhart and then popularized by Deming.

PFD: The letters stand for *process flow diagram*. A PFD is a type of flowchart that diagrams a process. Some organizations use the term *process map*.

prescriptive: The requirements are very specific and detailed. These types of requirements are not subject to wide interpretation.

procedure: 1. A document that provides information to carry out a process or activity in an orderly manner (the document can be in any medium). 2. A document that specifies a way to carry out an activity. 3. A set of steps that should be followed when seeking a desired effect.

process: 1. A set of interrelated or interacting activities that transforms inputs into outputs ANSI/ISO/ASQ Q9000. 2. A series of steps leading to a desired result. 3. A set or series of conditions, operations, or steps working together to produce a desired result.[21]

process audit: 1. An audit of the elements (conditions and resources) supporting an activity or process. 2. An analysis of a process and appraisal of completeness and correctness of the conditions with respect to some standard.[22] 3. An evaluation of established procedures.[23]

process control: When predetermined plans are followed, monitored against an acceptance criteria, and adjusted as needed to achieve objectives.

product: A product is the result of a process.[7] A product is normally thought to have physical, tangible properties (a mixer, a design report). A service may have intangible properties.

product audit: 1. An audit of a product or service (*see* audit). 2. Activity such as measuring, examining, testing, or gauging one or more characteristics of a product or service, done by an independent organization and comparing the results with specified requirements. 3. An independent examination of the characteristics and attributes of a product or service against a specification or acceptance criteria. 4. A quantitative assessment of conformance to required product characteristics.[22]

quality: 1. Degree to which a set of inherent characteristics fulfills requirements.[8] 2. Conformance to requirements. 3. Meeting customer requirements or achieving customer satisfaction.[19] 4. Quality for the supplier is getting it right the first time and quality for the customer is getting what he was expecting.[24]

quality audit: Systematic and independent examination to determine whether quality activities and related results comply with planned arrangements and whether these arrangements are implemented effectively and are suitable to achieve objectives.[25]

quality management: 1. Coordinated activities
to direct and control an organization with
regard to quality.[8] 2. Includes all activities
of the overall management function
(management system) that determines the
quality policy, objectives, and responsibilities
and their implementation.[10]

quality management system: A management
system to direct and control an organization
with regard to quality (ANSI/ISO/ASQ
Q9000-2000, clause 3.2.3).

record: 1. Data generated as a result of an
activity or process. A record can verify that
the activity took place. 2. A document stating
results achieved or providing evidence of
activities performed.[8]

reliability: Lack of unplanned failures or
shutdowns; that which one can depend upon.

Remedial (Containment) Action: An action
taken to alleviate the symptoms of existing
nonconformities or any other undesirable
situation. [J. P. Russell and Terry Regel, *After
the Quality Audit*, (Milwaukee: ASQ Quality
Press, 2000: 67.] Some standards

(ANSI/ISO/ASQ Q9000) use the term
correcting to describe superficial actions that
do not eliminate the cause of the problem.

requirement: Need or expectation that is stated,
generally implied, or obligatory.[7]

service: 1. A process. 2. A value-added activity
(value to the customer). 3. Intangible product
that is the result of at least one activity
performed at the interface between the
supplier and the customer. 4. The occupation
or function of serving. 5. Contribution to the
welfare of.

shall: The word *shall* is used in requirement or
contractual standards to indicate an absolute or
strict requirement. The words *must* and *will* are
also used to indicate an absolute or strict
requirement.

simple process audit: Auditing a process at the
work station or work instruction level. A
simple transformation, such as stamping,
painting, drilling, forming, reacting,
transacting, and so on.

strategic: 1. An adaptation or complex of
adaptations (as of behavior, metabolism,
or structure) that serves or appears to serve
an important function in achieving
evolutionary success. Of great importance
within an integrated whole or to a planned
effect (accessed on October 30, 2002 at
unabridged.merriam-webster.com/).
2. (a) necessary to or important in the
initiation, conduct, or completion of a
strategic plan; (b) of great importance within
an integrated whole or to a planned effect
(accessed October 21, 2002 at
www.yourdictionary.com).

suboptimal: Operating suboptimally is operating
below capacity of the process to achieve
objectives. Some processes are constrained
due to market conditions and operate
suboptimally. Some job designs are suboptimal
such as a retail store clerk standing around
waiting for the next customer to show up.
Suboptimal processes are responsible for
inefficiencies. Without a driving force, such as
profit, suboptimal operations are a natural state.

supplier: Organization or person that provides a
product or result of a process. For example:

retailer, distributor, manufacturer, and services.

system: 1. A group of processes supported by an infrastructure to manage and coordinate its function.[21] 2. A set of interrelated or interacting elements.[7]

system audit: An audit of a system. Sometimes called a quality audit or environmental audit.

systemic: Of, relating to, or common to a *system*. Systemic is something that is inherent in a process or system. A systemic problem will reoccur by design as opposed to a chance happening (isolated incident).

tactical: 1. Involving actions or means that are distinguished from those of strategy by being of less importance to the outcome or of less magnitude. Designed to achieve a given purpose (accessed on October 30, 2002 at unabridged.merriam-webster.com).
2. As (a) of or relating to small-scale actions serving a larger purpose; (b) made or carried out with only a limited or immediate end in view; (c) adroit in planning or maneuvering to accomplish a purpose (accessed October 21, 2002 at www.yourdictionary.com).

team: Two or more people working together to achieve a desired goal.

top box: Top box means the percent of respondents who marked either 4 or 5 on a five point Likert scale of satisfaction (1=very dissatisfied to 5=very satisfied). Top box is a more lenient measure of satisfied customers than just giving the percentage of those who marked 5.

top management: Person or group of people who directs and controls an organization at the highest level [ANSI/ISO/ASQ Q9000]. Synonyms are: executive, senior management, company officer, partner.

tracing: Audit tracing is following the chronological progress of a process. It is an effective means of collecting objective evidence. Forward tracing starts at the beginning; reverse (or backwards) tracing starts at the end and works toward the beginning.

work environment: A set of conditions under which work is performed.[7] For example:

temperature, lighting, pressure, humidity, space, psychological, stress, and so on.

work instructions: A document that provides detailed information to carry out a process, subprocess, or activity in a step-by-step manner (the document can be in any medium).

working papers: Documents, forms, checklists, or guidelines used by the auditor to help him/her perform an effective audit.

Endnotes

1. Olaf A. Houge, *Chemical Process Principles*, 2nd ed. (New York: John Wiley & Sons, 1965).
2. A concept shared with me by Dave Kildahl, Past Chair of the ASQ Quality Audit Division.
3. www.idef.com/idef3.html accessed on September 28, 2002, © 2000 KBSI.
4. J. P. Russell, *The Quality Audit Handbook* (Milwaukee: ASQ Quality Press, 2000): 185.
5. D. H. Besterfield, *Quality Control*, 5th ed. (Prentice-Hall, 1998).
6. J. M. Juran, *Juran's Quality Control Handbook*, 4th ed. (New York: McGraw-Hill, 1988).
7. ANSI/ISO/ASQ Q9000:2000, *Quality management systems—Fundamentals and vocabulary* (Milwaukee: ASQ Quality Press, 2000).
8. Ibid.
9. ISO/DIS 19011, Guidelines for quality and/or environmental management systems auditing (Geneva: International Organization for Standardization, 2001).
10. ANSI/ISO/ASQC A8402-1994., *Quality Management and Quality Assurance–Vocabulary* (Milwaukee: ASQ Quality Press, 1994); J. Muschlitz, *Quality Auditor Review Newsletter* 3, vol. 1 (1997): 4.
11. www.yourdictionary.com, accessed January 2002.

12. ISO/CD 14001, *Environmental management systems—Requirements with guidance for use* (Geneva: International Organization for Standardization, 2001).

13. Okes, D. and R. T. Westcott, eds., *The Certified Quality Manager Handbook*, 2nd. ed. (Milwaukee: ASQ Quality Press, 2001).

14. D. Hutton, *From Baldrige to the Bottom Line* (Milwaukee: ASQ Quality Press, 2000).

15. Russell, J. P., and T. Regel, *After the Quality Audit: Closing the Loop on the Audit Process*, 2nd ed. (Milwaukee: ASQ Quality Press, 2000): 116.

16. J. P. Russell, ed., *The Quality Audit Handbook*, 2nd ed. (Milwaukee: ASQ Quality Press, 2000)

17. Russell and Regel, *After the Quality Audit*, 113.

18. N. R. Tague, *The Quality Toolbox* (Milwaukee: ASQC Quality Press, 1995).

19. *Random House College Dictionary* (New York: Random House, 1988).

20. *American Heritage Dictionary*, 2nd ed. (Boston: Houghton Mifflin, 1985).

21. Russell and Regel, *After the Quality Audit*.

22. C. A. Mills, *The Quality Audit* (New York: McGraw-Hill, 1989).

23. B. S. Parsowith, *Fundamentals of Quality Auditing* (Milwaukee: ASQC Quality Press, 1995).

24. J. P. Russell, *The Quality Master Plan* (Milwaukee: ASQC Quality Press, 1990, now available from JP Russell & Associates, Gulf Breeze, FL).

25. ANSI/ISO/ASQC Q10011:1994. *Guidelines for Auditing Quality Systems* (Milwaukee: ASQ Quality Press, 1994).

For more advanced study, you may want to consider the following texts:

Arter, D. *Quality Audits for Improved Performance,* 3rd ed. Milwaukee: ASQ Quality Press, 1994.

Russell, J. P., and T. Regel. *After the Quality Audit.* Milwaukee: ASQ Quality Press, 2000.

Russell, J. P. *The Quality Audit Handbook.* Milwaukee: ASQ Quality Press, 2000.

Appendix A

IDEF Model Description

The IDEF3 Process Description Capture Method provides a mechanism for collecting and documenting processes. IDEF3 captures precedence and causality relations between situations and events in a form natural to domain experts by providing a structured method for expressing knowledge about how a system, process, or organization works. For more information about IDEF0, IDEF1, and IDEF3, explore the following references:

- www.idef.com

- www.micrografx.com/igrafx/idef0/

- type in IDEF0 or IDEF3 on your internet search engine

Appendix B

Process Control Checklist
(taken from ANSI/ISO/ASQ Q9001-2000
clause 7.5.1, used by permission.)

7.5.1	Control of product and service provision control	Okay?
7.5.1	Are provisions (product and service) carried out under controlled conditions?	
7.5.1-1	Is there product/service information available that describes product characteristics? [Acceptance criteria]	
7.5.1-2	Are there work instructions for activities necessary to achieve quality? (Where necessary)	
7.5.1-3	Is suitable equipment used on each of these identified processes (production, service)? [linked to 6.3 and 6.4]	
7.5.1-4	Are measurement and monitoring devices available and used? [Check the devices used to control the process]	
7.5.1-5	Are measuring and monitoring activities (processes) implemented?	
7.5.1-6	Are processes for release, delivery, and applicable post delivery implemented?	

Note: More comprehensive checklists may be required for second- and third-party audits.

Appendix C

Clause 4.1 Requirements

ANSI/ISO/ASQ Q9001-2000 clause 4.1 a) through
f) requirements are examined below.

Has the organization:

- Identified processes

- Determined the sequence and interaction
  of processes

- Determined criteria and methods to ensure
  effectiveness

- Ensured the availability of resources and
  information

- Determined the measuring, monitoring, and
  analyzing of these processes

- Implemented actions to achieve planned
  results and continual improvement

Process Approach

The process approach could have just as well been called the system approach. The key to successful implementation and auditing is ANSI/ISO/ASQ Q9001-2000 clause 4.1 Note.

ANSI/ISO/ASQ Q9001-2000 clause 4.1 Note:

Processes needed for the QMS referred to above should include processes for management activities, provision of resources, product realization and measurement.

Meaning there should be defined processes that meet clause 4.1 requirements for:

- Management activities (clause 5 includes management planning and review)

- Provision of resources (clause 6 includes training and infrastructure)

- Product realization (clause 7 includes everything from taking the order to providing the product)

- Measurement (clause 8 includes all the measurement processes)

Appendix D

Process Audit Report and Corrective Action Record

To:		Report Date:	Audit No.:
From:		Audit Date(s):	Auditor(s):Print and Initial
Copy:		Approved by:	
Process Audited:			
Purpose:			
Standard – Procedure – Instruction:			

Overall Findings/Conclusion:

Report Details

No.	Finding/Nonconformance	Ref # Para.	Follow-up Action Remedial and/or Corrective Action	Planned Completion Date	Status		
					Plan Approved	Actual Completion Date	Verified

Confidential

Appendix E

Standard Flowchart Symbols

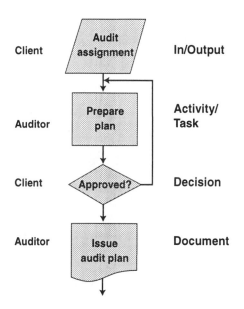

Appendix F

Example Process Map

Packaging – Process Map

Scope: The Packaging Department bags product from in-process silos. The department must comply with procedures 755-01, 755-03, and 755-10.

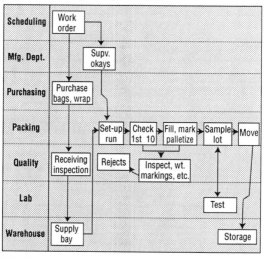

Note: The process map can be enhanced by adding clause or procedure numbers for each step.

Index